THE
EVERYTHING.
MORE MEMORY BOOSTER
PUZZLES BOOK

Dear Reader,

It's not often that something fun can also be good for us. As author of more than forty puzzle books, I like the idea that having fun with puzzles can be healthy. It seems like common sense to me: if we want to improve our memory, then we should exercise our brains by doing things like solving puzzles. A growing body of scientific research suggests that mental aerobics can be beneficial. Many people seem to agree—my first *Everything*® *Memory Booster Puzzles Book* was so successful that we decided to put together this new volume.

   I've filled this book with the very best puzzles. They were chosen because they are all really enjoyable and provide a diverse mental workout. I don't think a strenuous effort is required to effectively exercise our brains, so these puzzles are relatively easy, but they are challenging enough to provide plenty of those satisfying "aha!" moments when solutions are found. Have fun!

Charles Timmerman

Welcome to the EVERYTHING® Series!

These handy, accessible books give you all you need to tackle a difficult project, gain a new hobby, comprehend a fascinating topic, prepare for an exam, or even brush up on something you learned back in school but have since forgotten.

You can choose to read an *Everything*® book from cover to cover or just pick out the information you want from our four useful boxes: e-questions, e-facts, e-alerts, and e-ssentials. We give you everything you need to know on the subject, but throw in a lot of fun stuff along the way, too.

We now have more than 400 *Everything*® books in print, spanning such wide-ranging categories as weddings, pregnancy, cooking, music instruction, foreign language, crafts, pets, New Age, and so much more. When you're done reading them all, you can finally say you know *Everything*®!

PUBLISHER Karen Cooper

DIRECTOR OF ACQUISITIONS AND INNOVATION Paula Munier

MANAGING EDITOR, EVERYTHING® SERIES Lisa Laing

COPY CHIEF Casey Ebert

ACQUISITIONS EDITOR Lisa Laing

DEVELOPMENT EDITOR Brett Palana-Shanahan

EDITORIAL ASSISTANT Ross Weisman

EVERYTHING® SERIES COVER DESIGNER Erin Alexander

LAYOUT DESIGNERS Colleen Cunningham, Elisabeth Lariviere, Ashley Vierra, Denise Wallace

Visit the entire Everything® series at *www.everything.com*

THE EVERYTHING®

MORE MEMORY BOOSTER PUZZLES BOOK

Exercise your brain with
more than 250 challenging puzzles!

Charles Timmerman
Founder of Funster.com

Adams Media
New York London Toronto Sydney New Delhi

For Suzanne, Calla, and Meryl—
thanks for the memories!

Adams Media
An Imprint of Simon & Schuster, Inc.
57 Littlefield Street
Avon, Massachusetts 02322
Copyright © 2010 by Simon & Schuster, Inc.

An Everything® Series Book.
Everything® and everything.com® are registered trademarks of Simon & Schuster, Inc.

ADAMS MEDIA and colophon are trademarks of Simon and Schuster.

For information about special discounts for bulk purchases, please contact Simon & Schuster Special Sales at 1-866-506-1949 or business@simonandschuster.com.

The Simon & Schuster Speakers Bureau can bring authors to your live event. For more information or to book an event contact the Simon & Schuster Speakers Bureau at 1-866-248-3049 or visit our website at www.simonspeakers.com.

Manufactured in the United States of America

10

Library of Congress Cataloging-in-Publication Data has been applied for.

ISBN 978-1-4405-0555-3
ISBN 978-1-4405-0556-0 (ebook)

This publication is designed to provide accurate and authoritative information with regard to the subject matter covered. It is sold with the understanding that the publisher is not engaged in rendering legal, accounting, or other professional advice. If legal advice or other expert assistance is required, the services of a competent professional person should be sought.

—From a *Declaration of Principles* jointly adopted by a Committee of the American Bar Association and a Committee of Publishers and Associations

Many of the designations used by manufacturers and sellers to distinguish their products are claimed as trademarks. Where those designations appear in this book and Simon & Schuster, Inc., was aware of a trademark claim, the designations have been printed with initial capital letters.

Contents

Acknowledgments

I would like to thank each and every one of the more than half a million people who have visited my website, *www.funster.com*, to play word games and puzzles. You have shown me how much fun puzzles can be, and how addictive they can become!

It is always a pleasure to acknowledge my agent, Jacky Sach, whose help and expertise has been invaluable over the years.

Once again, it was a delight working with everyone at Adams Media. I particularly want to thank my editor, Lisa Laing, for so skillfully managing the many projects we have worked on together.

Funster and *What's in a Name?* are trademarks of Charles Timmerman.

Introduction

USE IT OR LOSE IT. Everyone knows that physical exercise can keep their bodies healthy—just ask any of the millions of people who regularly visit a health club. New research tells us that we can also keep our brains fit with regular mental exercise. That's what this book is all about: mental aerobics that can give your memory a boost.

You don't have to be a "puzzle person" to enjoy this book. The puzzles here are made to engage your brain, not to melt it down. It's similar to physical fitness where just walking can be beneficial—mountain climbing and marathon running are not required. The mental challenges here will lead you to those moments of creativity when your brain is perhaps building new pathways.

Why do you need to keep your brain mentally fit? Well, some people just want to confidently connect names to faces in social situations. Others want to reduce their number of "senior moments," a euphemism for episodes of forgetfulness, which can happen at any age. For all of us, mental ability is increasingly important to be successful in the world today. In this information age you need a sharp brain to keep yourself afloat in a flood of data.

The good news is that scientific research suggests that mental aerobics can give your brain a boost. According to a study in the journal *Nature*, you can actually build brain mass by attempting mentally challenging tasks. In this study, volunteers spent three months learning to juggle (a mentally challenging task). Using MRI brain scans, it was discovered that the participants' brains had increased in volume. When the participants gave up juggling, their brains shrank back to their previous sizes. This book won't teach you how to juggle, but it will present you with numerous brain-building challenges.

Many people believe that memory loss is inevitable as they age. Research indicates that this doesn't have to be the case. In a study published in the *Journal of the American Medical Association*, 2,802 participants age sixty-five and older received cognitive training for two hours per week for five weeks. A significant number of the participants improved their memory and cognitive abilities, and this improvement even persisted for two years after the training. Another study published in the *New England Journal of Medicine* found that people could reduce their risk of Alzheimer's disease by adding one mentally stimulating activity per week. Adding more activities, like working a crossword puzzle every day, was even better.

Research also points to lifestyle changes that can give your brain a boost. A healthy low-fat diet with lots of fruits and vegetables is important to keep your brain in peak condition. Staying physically fit benefits the brain, as well as the rest of the body. And reducing stress will cut down on the mental wear and tear that keeps your mind from working efficiently. Doing all of these things, in addition to the mental aerobics in this book, can help give your memory a boost.

Motivation is important, so have fun as you start your training with these puzzles. Hopefully you will look forward to the challenges. There is a diversity of puzzles in this book, and some you will enjoy more than others. Give them all a chance—the ones that are the most frustrating at the start might become the most satisfying once they are mastered. It is okay to pick and choose from your favorites, but be sure to cross-train with a variety of puzzles for the most effective brain workout.

Your memory will work best if you have a positive, confident attitude. You can remember if you think you can! Getting this book and working these puzzles is a great start in boosting your memory.

CHAPTER 1

Forget Me Nots

The puzzles in this chapter present a simple challenge: remember lists of random items. This might sound difficult at first, but it will become easy and fun when you use the link system. Perhaps you will discover secrets about how your memory works.

The Link System

The idea behind the link system is to make a mental chain out of the list of items to be remembered. This is done by associating each item in the list with the next item in some memorable way.

Example

Say you want to memorize this list of things:

- TREE
- WHEEL
- KNEE
- HOUSE
- HAT
- FERRY

To make your first link, you need to think of a mental image to associate TREE with WHEEL. This could be done by imagining a wheel sitting next to a tree—a logical choice, but not really a memorable one. Let your imagination go wild and think of a bunch of wheels racing up and down a tree like a racetrack. Or imagine a car with four trees in place of wheels (your imagination is not limited to only what is possible). These are things you would surely remember if you saw them in the real world. So actually "see" one of these images in your mind's eye. Now given TREE, you should think of WHEEL. The first link is made!

Here is the key: people remember unusual things; they forget ordinary things. So the more remarkable, absurd, and bizarre you can make your link images, the better! Creating these weird associations is the fun part. Let's continue with this example.

Next on the list, you need to link WHEEL and KNEE. Maybe imagine a tattoo of a wheel being etched onto your knee (ouch). Or imagine precariously trying to balance a giant wheel on your knee. Pick the image that seems most *absurd* and actually visualize it in your mind.

To link KNEE and HOUSE you could imagine a giant's knee crashing through the roof of your house. You have put *action* into your association to make it memorable.

Next, you could link HOUSE with HAT by imagining a giant hat on a house. Or maybe imagine a thousand hats being thrown into the air by all of the houses in town. In this example, *exaggeration* makes the images stand out. Imagine objects much bigger or more numerous than they really are.

For the last item in this example, you could link HAT with FERRY by imagining a ferry made from a giant hat. Or picture someone wearing a ferry as a hat! For this link, you have made an unforgettable image by *interchanging* the roles of the two items in an unusual way.

One more thing—you need to be able to remember the first item in this list, so link it to something relevant. You could associate your list with this book. So for example, TREE could be linked to this book by imagining a tree filled with copies of this book in place of leaves. Go ahead, pick a copy!

Tips

For a link to work best, the items should *interact* with each other. Don't just imagine the two items sitting next to each other; they should actually *do* something with each other. Also, include lots of *detail* in your images to help lock the mental pictures into your memory.

Remember, you must actually *see* the images in your mind. Just thinking of great ideas for link associations is not enough; you have to really picture them. Now go back through the example and take the time to see each association. Then close this book and run through the list going from link to link. You might be surprised how easy it is.

The link system will work best for you when you come up with your own images. The creative act of dreaming up these associations will help cement them into your memory, and it will be a good mental exercise. No one else needs to know about the strange associations you create, so set your mind free and marvel at the bizarre images that will come forth! Children have no problem creating these kinds of silly pictures in their heads. With a little practice, your imagination will be back to where it was in grade school.

Forget Me Nots

Use the link system and create a memorable image for each neighboring pair. Vividly see each image in your mind's eye. As a check, immediately see if you can remember each item by running through all the links without looking. Then later in the day, or perhaps the next day, try to remember each item without looking at the list. You should even be able to run through a Forget Me Not list backward by using the links in reverse. Almost like mediation, thinking through a Forget Me Not list can be relaxing!

You will probably get faster at memorizing the lists as you get more experienced associating word pairs. This is a good thing, and it shows that your mind is more able to focus. If you want, use a timer to see how fast you can memorize a list.

These Forget Me Not puzzles are not meant to be done all at once. After you remember a Forget Me Not list, work other puzzles in this book. Then return to this chapter and see if you can still remember the list. You might get better at the Forget Me Not lists as your brain gets a workout from the other puzzles in this book. For more of a challenge, see if you can remember two or more of these lists by linking them together.

Forget Me Not Challenge 1

flame	flower
comb	change
bridge	cord
machine	key
water	collar

Forget Me Not Challenge 2

plough	tongue
blade	chin
cake	needle
skirt	cheese
pump	wall

Forget Me Not Challenge 3

nut	potato
hospital	daughter
sail	father
basket	paste
milk	spoon

Forget Me Not Challenge 1

_____ _____

_____ _____

_____ _____

_____ _____

_____ _____

Forget Me Not Challenge 2

_____ _____

_____ _____

_____ _____

_____ _____

_____ _____

Forget Me Not Challenge 3

_____ _____

_____ _____

_____ _____

_____ _____

_____ _____

Forget Me Not Challenge 4

bulb	feather
air	copper
ink	sign
root	ticket
soap	moon

Forget Me Not Challenge 5

space	ornament
coat	brain
edge	island
orange	church
heart	ring

Forget Me Not Challenge 6

family	engine
garden	watch
foot	prison
goat	wire
cloud	rice

Forget Me Not Challenge 4

_____   _____

_____   _____

_____   _____

_____   _____

_____   _____

Forget Me Not Challenge 5

_____   _____

_____   _____

_____   _____

_____   _____

_____   _____

Forget Me Not Challenge 6

_____   _____

_____   _____

_____   _____

_____   _____

_____   _____

Forget Me Not Challenge 7

thread	mouth
flag	secretary
match	test
bee	fruit
wind	girl

Forget Me Not Challenge 8

eye	square
curve	stick
shelf	pencil
hand	station
land	berry

Forget Me Not Challenge 9

ear	mountain
card	ship
insect	cork
rod	ice
wood	rain

Forget Me Not Challenge 7

_____   _____

_____   _____

_____   _____

_____   _____

_____   _____

Forget Me Not Challenge 8

_____   _____

_____   _____

_____   _____

_____   _____

_____   _____

Forget Me Not Challenge 9

_____   _____

_____   _____

_____   _____

_____   _____

_____   _____

Forget Me Not Challenge 10

money	parcel
glove	story
sock	gun
step	cushion
pen	soup

Forget Me Not Challenge 11

arch	room
powder	stomach
gold	dust
cat	fork
board	glass

Forget Me Not Challenge 12

knife	record
poison	curtain
bird	cart
stocking	drink
fire	boat

Forget Me Not Challenge 10

_____ _____

_____ _____

_____ _____

_____ _____

_____ _____

Forget Me Not Challenge 11

_____ _____

_____ _____

_____ _____

_____ _____

_____ _____

Forget Me Not Challenge 12

_____ _____

_____ _____

_____ _____

_____ _____

_____ _____

Forget Me Not Challenge 13

net	brick
grip	hook
drawer	hair
cotton	earth
door	star

Forget Me Not Challenge 14

box	drop
trousers	band
blood	toe
boy	worm
tooth	wave

Forget Me Not Challenge 15

leather	spring
dress	army
verse	tree
building	pot
farm	stage

Forget Me Not Challenge 13

_____   _____

_____   _____

_____   _____

_____   _____

_____   _____

Forget Me Not Challenge 14

_____   _____

_____   _____

_____   _____

_____   _____

_____   _____

Forget Me Not Challenge 15

_____   _____

_____   _____

_____   _____

_____   _____

_____   _____

Forget Me Not Challenge 16

plane	friend
hole	brush
library	kettle
bottle	train
umbrella	hat

Forget Me Not Challenge 17

neck	brake
bed	oven
oil	bell
roof	skin
sea	smile

Forget Me Not Challenge 18

pig	lip
line	whip
head	camera
man	knot
angle	art

Forget Me Not Challenge 16

_____   _____

_____   _____

_____   _____

_____   _____

_____   _____

Forget Me Not Challenge 17

_____   _____

_____   _____

_____   _____

_____   _____

_____   _____

Forget Me Not Challenge 18

_____   _____

_____   _____

_____   _____

_____   _____

_____   _____

CHAPTER 2

Crossword Puzzles

Studies have shown that doing crossword puzzles is a great way to keep your brain young. Give the puzzles in this chapter your best shot. It's okay if you can't fill in every entry, you will still be getting a good mental workout.

Crossword Puzzle 1

Across

3. Cherry seed
6. Playwright David
8. "No bid," in bridge
11. Jump on one foot
12. Singers Hall and ___
13. Dots in the ocean
16. Clothing
18. Traveler's reference
19. Move in the breeze
21. Sept. preceder
22. Not in class
26. Americans, to Brits
28. Appraiser
30. ET's transport
32. Skirt bottoms
33. Screwdriver, e.g.
36. Deuce beaters
38. After-Christmas event
39. Rank above cpl.
42. "Now it's clear"
43. Barnyard clucker
44. Venus de___
46. Caruso or Domingo
47. Not wide

Down

1. Love, to Pavarotti
2. Game show host Sajak
3. Hushed "Hey you!"
4. Spicy Asian cuisine
5. Rapid
7. Lean slightly
8. Letter before kappa
9. Doesn't fail
10. Close, as an envelope
14. Noticed
15. Isle of exile for Napoleon
17. Helpers for profs
20. Capone and Pacino
21. Major League brothers' name
23. Roof support
24. No, to Nikita
25. Picture card
27. Curly cabbages
28. Chapter and ___
29. Future attorney's exam: abbr.
31. Like Rapunzel's hair
34. Astronomical hunter
35. Deplete, with "up"
37. Calendar periods
40. Chew
41. On, as a lamp
43. Billy Joel's "Tell ___ About It"
45. Martial arts expert Bruce

Solution on page 144

Crossword Puzzle 2

Across

1. Roasts' hosts
4. Storytelling uncle of fiction
7. Electric power network
8. House extension
10. Bear's abode
12. One who mimics
15. Sufficient
16. Gala gathering
18. Place for a keystone
20. French holy woman: abbr.
21. Has some success
23. Far-flying seabird
26. "Nightline" host Koppel
27. ___ Kett of old comics
30. ___ support (computer help)
32. Makeshift shelter
33. Average mark
35. Basketball hoop
36. Notes after mis
37. Title for Churchill
38. ___ room (play area)
39. Paul who sang "Puppy Love"
40. Road topper

Down

1. Ron of "Tarzan"
2. Stockholm's country
3. Metal in rocks
4. Theme park attraction
5. Hosiery problem
6. Deuce, in tennis
7. Trimmed beard
9. Soap-making substances
11. Piece of pasta
13. Terrible twos, for one
14. Boulder
16. Duffer's cry
17. March 17 honoree, for short
19. Went by taxi
22. Guiding philosophy
24. Silently understood
25. Summer: Fr.
28. Holier-___-thou
29. Walrus features
31. Ship's staff
34. Clear the chalkboard
36. Raise crops

Solution on page 144

Crossword Puzzle 3

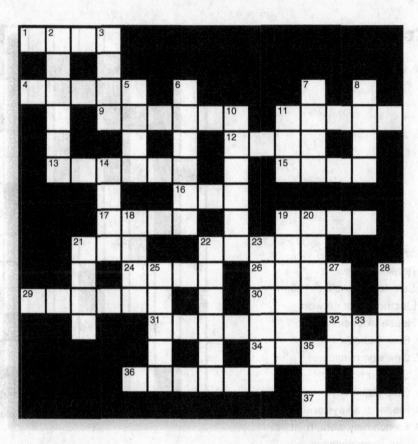

Across

1. Southwest Indian
4. Soprano Callas
9. Devious plot
11. Sir, in Seville
12. Shootout time, maybe
13. Justice ___ Day O'Connor
15. Women in habits
16. Addition result
17. Net material
19. Moslem cleric
21. 4:00 social
22. Part of UV
24. Self-absorbed
26. Ventilates, with "out"
29. English cathedral city
30. "What ___ become of me?"
31. Store, as grain
32. Wall Street index, with "the"
34. Movie awards
36. Headline
37. Canceled, as a launch

Down

2. Missouri mountains
3. Wader with a curved bill
5. The "A" in DNA
6. Clean again
7. Restaurant list
8. Hope and Barker
10. Tooth protector
11. Dad, to Grandpa
14. Tattle on
18. Roof's edge
19. Garden flowers
20. Retail store
21. Every now and ___
22. A choir may sing in it
23. Clothes alterer
25. Boxing site
27. Scotch mixer
28. Six o'clock broadcast
33. Not a duplicate: abbr.
35. Not pro

Solution on page 144

Crossword Puzzle 4

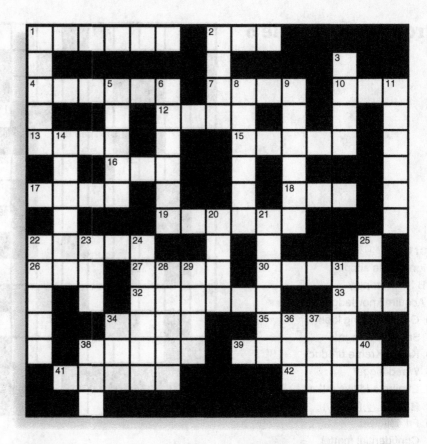

Across

1. Loewe's Broadway partner
2. Kid's question
4. Open with a key
7. Took a photo of
10. Hard-boiled item
12. West Coast wine valley
13. 50/50 share
15. Go on a buying spree
16. ___ and vinegar
17. Cow's hurdle, in rhyme
18. Tell a fib
19. Water absorber
22. ___ and true
26. Find a sum
27. Lighten, as a burden
30. Scarlett's spouse
32. Part of the eye
33. State west of Mont.
34. Pepsi or RC
35. Put on weight
38. Loses brightness
39. ___ bender (minor accident)
41. "___ and the Wolf"
42. Sing in the Alps

Down

1. Enjoy a joke
2. Hornet, e.g.
3. Plant's beginning
5. Go ___ a tangent
6. Mounds
8. Hightail it
9. ___ clef
11. Bodega owner
14. On ship
20. Unseal
21. Auto repair shop
22. Jobs to do
23. Driver's lic. and such

24. Translate, in a way
25. Part of PST: abbr.
28. "You've got mail" addressee
29. Spanish ladies: abbr.
31. Having prongs
34. Tabby
36. At ___ rate
37. Altar vows
38. FBI agent
40. Minister: abbr.

Solution on page 144

Crossword Puzzle 5

Across

1. Ignore the script
4. Bit of wordplay
6. Acquire knowledge
10. Give a longing look
11. Salon colorings
13. Krispy Kreme product
14. Weed digger
15. Engine additive letters
18. Raisin ___ (cereal)
19. Fri. follower
21. Confidential matter
24. Former Fed chief Greenspan
27. Left, at sea
28. Teeter-totter
31. Bronco-riding event
33. Restroom, informally
34. Element in salt
36. Dad's brother
37. Oxen coupler
39. Sothern and Jillian
40. Escalator alternative
41. Movie star's rep
42. Democratic Party symbol
43. Pitching great Tom

Down

2. Sags
3. Winter footwear
5. One: Fr.
7. Fire-setting crime
8. Scent detector
9. Hacienda material
12. Seuss turtle
16. Pre-1917 Russian ruler
17. Group of five
20. Record on video
22. Streets: Abbr.
23. Open courtyard
25. In need of tightening

26. Bygone airline
29. Television awards
30. Declare in court
32. Conduits
35. Rustic lodgings
38. Broadway performer
39. Pretentiously showy

Solution on page 144

Crossword Puzzle 6

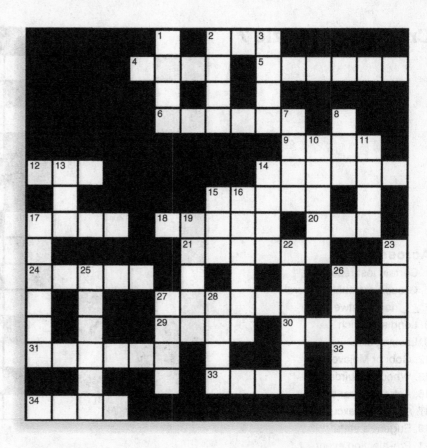

Across

2. Coffee-break time
4. Drive or reverse
5. Geometric figure with equal angles
6. Hole for a lace
9. Yeses at sea
12. Letters after els
14. Plaza Hotel heroine
15. ___ Way galaxy
17. Winter precipitation
18. "You can ___ horse to . . . "
20. Gives a thumbs-up
21. Dentists' tools
24. Spelling or Burr
26. Roam (about)
27. Radio interference
29. Letter carriers' grp.
30. Hospital area: abbr.
31. South Dakota's capital
32. Disappoint, with "down"
33. Encl. with a manuscript
34. Have a bite

Down

1. Roll-call call
2. Not false
3. Cairo's waterway
7. Have a chat
8. Luau garland
10. Duncan toys
11. Georgia and Ukraine, once: abbr.
13. Stag party attendees
14. Airline that serves only kosher food
15. Month after Feb.
16. Dolts
17. Get all sudsy
19. Prepares for publication
22. Transparent plastic
23. Adjusts to fit
25. Leaf collectors
26. Charles de ___
27. Mideast canal
28. Tarzan's raisers

Solution on page 144

Crossword Puzzle 7

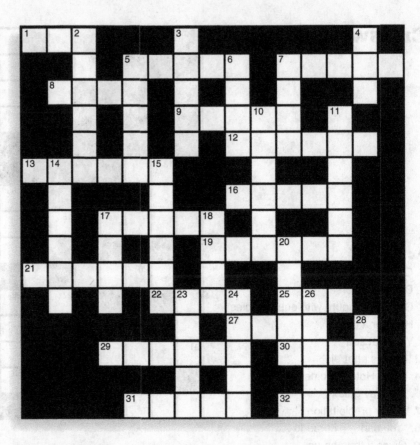

Across

1. Certain test results
5. Groups of troublemakers
7. ___ nous (between us)
8. Long sandwich
9. Lacking skill
12. Gobi or Mojave
13. Whooping birds
16. Actress Sarandon
17. Accused's excuse
19. Eugene's state
21. Pre-election event
22. Comical Laurel
25. "Leaving ___ Vegas"
27. Building annexes
29. Brother of Prince Charles
30. Where the Reds and the Browns play
31. Kasparov's game
32. On an ocean liner

Down

2. "A Streetcar Named Desire" woman
3. Calcutta's home
4. Lacking moisture
5. Golden-egg layer
6. Santa's vehicle
7. Stops fasting
10. Leaf through
11. Actor Hume
14. Fixes Junior's laces
15. Treats with malice
17. "Stronger than dirt" sloganeer
18. Des Moines is its capital
20. Winemaker Ernest or Julio
23. Stooges count
24. Brilliantly colored salamanders
26. Fireplace remnants
28. Lotus position discipline

Solution on page 145

Crossword Puzzle 8

Across

1. Head over heels
3. Airshow stunt
5. G-man's employer
6. Ancient Greek city
7. Like ghost stories
10. Scented pouch
14. Boring routines
16. Rat (on)
17. Miami basketball team
18. French ___ soup
19. Three feet
20. A.k.a. Bruins
22. "Now we're in trouble!"
23. Writer of rhymes
24. Pharmaceutical
25. Suffix with lemon or lime
26. German author Hermann
29. Money in Mexico
31. ___ upon a time
32. Broadcast's sound portion
35. One named in a will
36. Pacific weather phenomenon
37. Prefers
38. Highlands girl

Down

1. "___ no kick from Champagne"
2. Be defeated
3. Dog's restraint
4. Desserts with crusts
5. Mink or sable
8. Soothed
9. Calendar girl
10. Part of Congress
11. Boxer Muhammad
12. Sun blockers
13. However
14. Synthetic fibers
15. Salt Lake state
16. Ohio port
21. Part of USCG
27. Hits the "Send" button
28. The Four Hundred
29. Tree with cones
30. ___ a happy note
33. "Mila 18" novelist
34. Three, on a sundial

Solution on page 145

Crossword Puzzle 9

Across

1. Meal starter, often
3. "Schindler's List" star Liam
8. Eve's second son
10. Brittle cookie
12. Gloomy ___
13. Poker pot primer
15. Extends a subscription
17. Trio after R
18. Beard remover
19. Luxuriant, as vegetation
24. Goes out, as a fire
26. Spud
27. Salacious glance
28. Put up on eBay
30. Pointed a pistol
31. Hamilton bills
32. Astute
35. Put in the bank
38. Office helper: abbr.
40. Physically weak
41. "Golden touch" king
42. Bathroom hanger
43. Enjoy the taste of

Down

1. T-bone or porterhouse
2. On a liner
4. Snail-like
5. Remind too often
6. Annoyers
7. Christmas songs
9. Greyhound vehicle
11. Llama's land
14. Baseball deals
16. Sound in a cave
20. Used up, as money
21. Actress Tomei
22. Bluto's rival

23. Clears snow from
25. Actress Worth
29. Jar tops
30. Question's opposite: abbr.
33. Cattle groups
34. Ralph ___ Emerson
36. Bit of bridal attire
37. Handed out cards
39. "The Wizard of Oz" dog
41. "Oh, give ___ home . . ."

Solution on page 145

Crossword Puzzle 10

Across

1. Pizzeria fixtures
3. Mattress filling
4. 7, on a sundial
8. In high style
12. Hair-setting item
15. Comment ending
17. Ocean bottoms
19. "Sesame Street" regular
21. "___-di-dah!"
22. One who calls balls
24. Topic for Dr. Ruth
25. Back-breaking dance
26. "The Canterbury ___"
29. Knight titles
30. Shamu or Keiko
31. Suffix with north or south
33. Sedan or coupe
35. Boll eater
36. PhD exams
38. Actress May
39. Evil woman
40. Really impress

Down

1. "___ Twist"
2. Sound thinking
5. Just sitting around
6. Mental quickness
7. Accelerator or brake
9. Trunk fastener
10. Snake charmers' snakes
11. Fence openings
13. Put on the payroll again
14. Half a ticket
16. Fishing line holder
18. Med. care choices
20. Talmud language
23. Modest response to a compliment
27. Online letter
28. Leaf-gathering tool
32. Parts in plays
34. Angry feeling
36. Early afternoon hour
37. Scatter seed

Solution on page 145

Crossword Puzzle 11

Across

1. Mr. Claus
4. Spring or summer
7. Liquid rock
9. Back, at sea
10. Ugly duckling, ultimately
11. Read superficially
12. "Charlotte's ___"
14. Normandy campaign town
16. Above, in poetry
17. Red gem
19. ___ borealis (northern lights)
21. Many Mideasterners
22. Duo
23. ___ Canaveral
24. Get groceries
26. Ten years
29. ___ Lee (cake company)
31. Chauffeured vehicle
32. Acorn product
33. Lunch meat
34. Eskimo dwelling
35. Blossom
36. Opposite of max.
37. "___ Are My Sunshine"

Down

2. Tiny hill dwellers
3. Texas battle site of 1836
4. Emphatic assent in Acapulco
5. Detection device
6. Hammer's target
8. Woodchopper's tool
12. Christmas garland
13. Bridge calls
15. Gave a speech
18. Unbroken horse
19. Opera solos
20. "Gone With the Wind" surname
24. Not very often
25. Nonpoetic writing
27. Igloo dweller
28. Bride's walkway
30. Elbow's site
32. Yoko of music
33. Horse food

Solution on page 145

Crossword Puzzle 12

Across

4. Bite like a pup
5. Go on all fours
6. Bambi and others
8. Brazilian ballroom dance
10. Actor George C.
11. Adam and Eve locale
13. Asner and Wynn
15. "Peter, Peter, Pumpkin ___"
18. Eiffel Tower city
20. Cave dwellers
22. Fictional work
24. Sly animal
25. ___ out a living (just gets by)
27. It's south of Ga.
28. Attaches, as a rope
29. Mil. entertainment group
31. Chocolate candy
33. Sound like a fan
34. X and Y on a graph
37. Blouse or shirt
39. Legal rights grp.
40. Cain's eldest son
41. River blocker
42. Good for what ___ you
43. Lawyers: abbr.

Down

1. Captain Kidd, for one
2. One of the five senses
3. North Pole toymaker
4. Home on a branch
5. Nickel or dime
6. Physicians, for short
7. Help a hoodlum
9. Very skilled
12. Clears the blackboard
14. Has the helm
16. Monastery heads
17. Sheets, tablecloths, etc.
19. Morse code message

21. X or Y, on a graph
23. Lobster's grabber
26. Where Seoul is
30. Rowing need
31. High-flying toys
32. De-wrinkle
35. "Get lost, kitty!"
36. Bombs that don't explode
38. "The Murders in the Rue Morgue" writer

Solution on page 145

Crossword Puzzle 13

Across

1. Prayer's end
2. Home audio system
7. In the ___ of luxury
9. Happy ___ lark
11. Collar, as a crook
13. Keep an ___ to the ground
15. Headache helper
18. Wild times
19. Judge's gown
20. Tennis champ Arthur
22. Scone spread
23. It replaced the lira
24. Eve's man
27. 1950s candidate Kefauver
29. Family friendly, in cinema
32. Winding road shape
34. Abbr. before an alias
36. College website letters
38. Lawful, for short
39. School support org.
41. Road divisions
42. Ascots
44. Bricks measure
45. Boundary
47. Party attendees

Down

1. Palestinian leader
3. Oompah instrument
4. Sleep phenomenon: abbr.
5. Song from the past
6. Not near
8. Household animal
10. Atmosphere
11. Omaha's state: abbr.
12. Lincoln or Vigoda
14. Houston baseballers
16. Baseball great Ty
17. Sal of song, e.g.
18. ___ Scholar

21. The Caribbean, e.g.
23. Ambulance driver, for short
25. Desirable qualities
26. Gets well
28. Blow, volcano-style
30. Lacking a key, in music
31. Comedian's bit
32. Restaurant activity
33. Not true
35. Paper-and-string flier
37. Mover's vehicle
40. Light throw
43. Part of HEW: abbr.
46. Dream Team jersey letters

Solution on page 146

Crossword Puzzle 14

Across

1. Beauty queen's crown
5. Irish or English dog
7. Deepen, as a canal
8. Store goods: abbr.
12. Exxon product
14. Sheriff's sidekick
15. Foot the bill
17. Like an antique
18. Large coffee maker
19. Hangs on a clothesline
21. Channel for armchair athletes
23. Enjoy some gum
24. Pee Wee of Ebbets Field
29. Pepsi competitor
32. Director De Palma
34. Peas' home
35. Not happy
36. Reverberations

Down

1. Boy king of ancient Egypt
2. Noun modifier: abbr.
3. Be very fond of
4. Have a look

5. Made a smooth transition
6. Your, in the Bible
9. Ten dimes
10. "Rabbit, Run" author
11. Nuclear experiments
13. Shopper's binge
16. Response
19. '50s presidential monogram
20. Monkey Trial name
22. Drug agent, slangily
25. Filled with joy
26. Cry loudly
27. Added to the payroll
28. Corporation abbr.

30. Lifesaving skill, for short
31. Pindar poem
33. RNs' coworkers

Solution on page 146

Crossword Puzzle 15

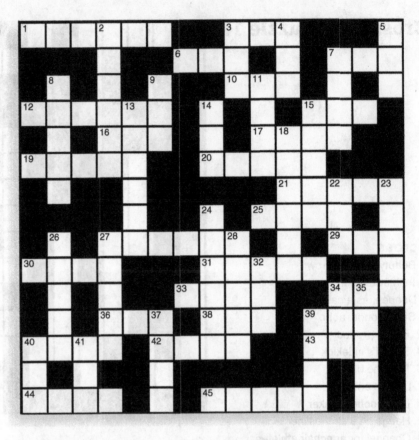

Across

1. Backs of boats
3. Soft food for infants
6. Tire pressure meas.
7. Birmingham's state: abbr.
10. Flow's counterpart
12. Reveal, as a secret
15. Bath site
16. "___ be darned!"
17. Light bulb, in cartoons
19. Likely (to)
20. Colorado ski town
21. Two-___ (deceitful)
25. Peru's largest city
27. In a chair
29. Office seeker, for short
30. Locker room powder
31. Swatch competitor
33. ___ Major (constellation)
34. Lousy grade
36. Amount after expenses
38. Highest card
39. Use a microwave
40. Overpublicize
42. Remove, as a knot
43. Magazine fillers
44. Aspiration
45. Stitched lines

Down

2. Sign up, with again
3. Fruit-filled dessert
4. Place to play darts
5. Cartographer's product
7. Color of water
8. Put out, as effort
9. Hair stiffener
11. Radar screen spot
13. Vulgar person
14. Squeezing snake
15. Two hours before noon
18. Give the meaning of
22. Beanie
23. Fellini's "La ___ Vita"
24. Group of four
26. Every 24 hours
27. Act segment
28. Place to do the hustle
32. West of old films
34. Mom's partner
35. England's ___ Downs
37. Surf and ___
39. Cooks in a microwave
40. "What'd you say?"
41. Break, as a balloon

Solution on page 146

CHAPTER 3

Sudoku Puzzles

Sudoku burst onto the world stage in 2005 and continues to grow in popularity. Perhaps one of the secrets to its success is the puzzle's charming simplicity. Sudoku is played on a 9 × 9 grid. Heavier lines subdivide this grid into nine 3 × 3 boxes. The object is to fill in the grid so that every row, column, and 3 × 3 box contains the numbers one through nine with no repeats. The puzzle begins with some of the numbers already entered. There will always be just one solution for each puzzle.

Sudoku Puzzle 1

	1		8	7	3		4	
9			1		2			
5	8					7		
				3			6	4
6								9
4	3			9				
		4					8	6
			6		7			3
		6		3	4	1	7	

Sudoku Puzzle 2

		8	4		9		7	
4	1							
3				8				
5			3				2	1
9			4					5
2	6		8					9
			3					4
							5	7
	5		7		1	3		

Solution on page 147

Sudoku Puzzle 3

6		2	5	3				
	3						9	
7	8		2		1			
			4			7		5
5								9
4		8		3				
			9		8		5	7
	5						1	
			7	5	2			8

Sudoku Puzzle 4

3		4						5
			7	2		9		
							1	
1			8				5	6
	5			1			2	
7	8			2				4
	4							
		1		7	3			
2						3		9

Solution on page 147

Sudoku Puzzle 5

8		5	2	1				6
	3		6			8		
		1						
				9	4	3		
		8				6		
		4	5	7				
						7		
		3			7		8	
7				6	1	4		9

Sudoku Puzzle 6

6					1			8
			4					
4	1				7		2	
5			8	6	2			3
				4				
2			3	7	9			6
	7		6				5	4
				8				
3			9					2

Solution on page 147

Sudoku Puzzle 7

3	5	6	8		7			
8			5				9	
1								
	6			1		3		
5		2				8		9
		1		5			6	
								4
	4				5			3
		7		4	6	5	1	

Sudoku Puzzle 8

8	5		9		4			
							8	7
4							9	3
		4		6			7	
6			7		3			4
	3			5		9		
9	1							6
5	6							
			6		8		5	2

Solution on page 148

Sudoku Puzzle 9

4	2	5	7			6		
6								
	3	7		2				
1	7			9	3			5
5								8
2			1	8			3	6
				7		8	6	
								4
		4			8	5	1	2

Sudoku Puzzle 10

8	3	9	4			7	5	
	2				3			
1			7	6				
						2		
		3		5		1		
		6						
				3	4			1
			9				8	
	7	5			8	3	9	2

Solution on page 148

Sudoku Puzzle 11

	1	5				3	6	
				8				
9					4			1
1		2	5			3		
			9	6	1			
		6			8	5		7
3			7					4
				1				
		7	4				1	6

Sudoku Puzzle 12

			7					9
		9		2	3	6		1
	5						4	
	8		3	9	1			
1								3
			4	8	7		5	
	3						9	
6		1	8	7		4		
4					6			

Solution on page 148

Sudoku Puzzle 13

```
. 7 . | 3 . . | 5 9 .
. 5 9 | 8 . 1 | . . 2
. . 3 | . . . | . . .
------+-------+------
. . . | 4 . . | 3 . .
. . 6 | 1 . . | 8 . .
. . 5 | . . 7 | . . .
------+-------+------
. . . | . . . | 2 . .
6 . . | 5 . . | 8 9 7
. 1 4 | . . 3 | . 5 .
```

Sudoku Puzzle 14

```
. . 4 | 3 7 . | . . .
2 . . | 9 4 . | . 1 .
. 6 . | . . . | 7 . 4
------+-------+------
5 . . | . . . | . . .
. . 9 | 6 . 5 | 2 . .
. . . | . . . | . . 1
------+-------+------
9 . 5 | . . . | 8 . .
. 7 . | . 5 1 | . . 2
. . . | 4 8 . | 1 . .
```

Solution on page 149

Sudoku Puzzle 15

		8		9			5	
3		9	4					7
	4	5						
6	5				9	7		
		3	6		7	2		
		7	5				9	6
						4	2	
5					4	8		3
	2			6		5		

Sudoku Puzzle 16

	5	8		2			6	
3			4		6			5
				8				
7						4	9	
5			8	3	9			2
	1	9						3
			2					
1			6		3			9
	6			8		1	4	

Solution on page 149

Sudoku Puzzle 17

5		1		6	4			
7	9			8				
8		2					3	
			5		9		6	
			1	7	6			
	2		4		8			
	1					7		5
				5			4	2
			7	4		3		6

Sudoku Puzzle 18

	2				4	3	1	
	1		5	8				
9				3				
					8	1		
		4				2		
		8	9					
				4				5
				7	1		8	
	8	6	2				9	

Solution on page 149

Sudoku Puzzle 19

2		3	6				5	7
6	5							
1						6	3	
4			5	2				
		1	3		8	7		
				4	7			6
	3	6						8
							7	9
8	1				5	4		2

Sudoku Puzzle 20

4		9	7					
5		1		2	4			7
				1	3			
9							2	3
7				5				6
2	6							4
			1	9				
8			5	3		4		1
				8	9			2

Solution on page 150

Sudoku Puzzle 21

			2		8		4	1
		8				7	5	6
						8		
6	3	4	8			9		
			9		7			
		9			1	4	8	5
		3						
9	7	6				5		
4	1		3		5			

Sudoku Puzzle 22

			4	3		7		
3						5	6	
9		8			5			4
			1			6		
		1	8		6	2		
		5		3				
5			1			4		7
	4	6						9
		9	4	5				

Solution on page 150

Sudoku Puzzle 23

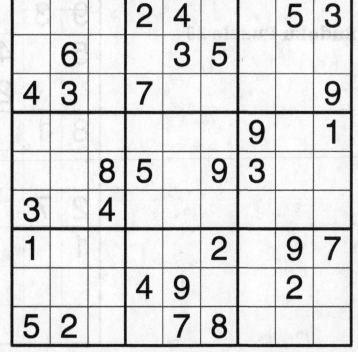

Sudoku Puzzle 24

Solution on page 150

Sudoku Puzzle 25

2				5	9	6		1
	9			2			7	
7						2		3
8			3		5			
				8				
			9		2			7
6		8						2
	3			1			8	
4		2	8	9				6

Sudoku Puzzle 26

9	3							
5		4	9		6			
		2			5			4
8	1			7			2	5
2	7			5			3	1
1			2			6		
			5		4	9		3
							5	2

Solution on page 151

Sudoku Puzzle 27

4			7				2	
5	1							
9		2		8				3
2			8			9		
	4		1		6		5	
		5			4			6
7				1		3		2
							6	7
	3				2			1

Sudoku Puzzle 28

			3		4			5
				2				3
1				6				8
	2			5			3	
		6	2		3	8		
	4			8			1	
8				3				4
6				1				
9			8		5			

Solution on page 151

Sudoku Puzzle 29

8	9	2	1					3
	5							
6		1		4				
1		7		6	9		4	
				7				
	3		4	8		6		2
				2		9		7
							1	
3					5	8	2	4

Sudoku Puzzle 30

1	3				2		4	8
8		6	3					
4			9	8				
	4		2				7	
		8				4		
	1				3		9	
				1	9			7
					7	3		9
9	2		6				8	4

Solution on page 151

CHAPTER 4

Word Search Puzzles

The puzzles in this chapter are in the traditional word search format. Words are hidden in a grid in any direction: up, down, forward, backward, or diagonally. The words are always found in a straight line, and letters are never skipped. Words can overlap. For example, the letters at the end of the word MAST could be used as the start of the word STERN. Only the letters A to Z are used, and any spaces in an entry are removed. For example, TROPICAL FISH would be found in the grid as TROPICALFISH.

Drink Up

```
R X H B H P P J M Y Q E C S P I M T N U
H L J O W M U W N R N T L H S A G E N R
B R M X J U Q N C R E B S P R T R A Q P
O D E G B S Y R C E C U E T P I A N R L
T N K O T C E R W H R P I I R A P J Q W
T Q O R O A D S A C D N K M T M E R B Z
L Z C G M T A B G M I E O L L W J N N O
E N M S A R N W L R Y U T G T I U A I Y
N E O W T S O G R A N D M A R N I E R P
G D O U O C M J S T C U O I N S C R X K
A L N W J R E N A N L K S O S O E D L W
P Z S R U E L I A L I H R U L B B I P H
M R H J I W N A E T C L R U P B M R I X
A O I X C D S D L O T E L S S R T G A E
H H N C E R W E F I T A A O E S H P Z C
C F E W E I O F I I Q R H T C B I A G H
A U X T N V E B H N L U T N A M D A T A
M D T E A E T W R B L U E L A G O O N S
Y I B O U R B O N O B Q L U J M D T G E
B J Z C Y P H D F G Y W P F R E S C A R
```

BITTERS

BLACK RUSSIAN

BLOODY MARY

BLUE LAGOON

BOOZE

BOTTLE

BOURBON

BUTTERMILK

CARBONATED

CHAMPAGNE

CHASER

CHERRY

COKE

CREAM SODA

CRUSH

FRESCA

GRAND MARNIER

GRAPE JUICE

GROG

HIGHBALL

IRISH COFFEE

LEMONADE

LIQUEUR

MAI TAI

MANHATTAN

MARTINI

MOONSHINE

MOUNTAIN DEW

MULLED WINE

MUSCAT

NUTRASWEET

PEPSI

PINEAPPLE

PUNCH

RASPBERRY

ROB ROY

SCREWDRIVER

TOM COLLINS

TOMATO JUICE

WHITE RUSSIAN

Solution on page 152

Beautiful Music

```
J Z C U G B L I O H T O O M S M H A R B
F O Z H W X E M I L T J A C K S O N B R
S L H A F S A N O R K C O D A Y O F A I
Y E E N J E H L N I V D H R J D D G T T
V V P O N N C O A Y T I R I W O N T O T
T I I I N Y I N S N G T N U M L E J N E
I B C C P A M T A T J O A G M E C I O N
M R O U T G R E A M A A O L B M S O I O
P A N E S I A D R L R K Y D R E E O T T
A P G K N W C B B C V O O L M A R R A N
N H A G O B Y C P E E V F V E A C L S E
I O S S I N G I N G R R O R I R N S I K
S N R T U B A Z O A N N F I E C N G V N
E E N O H P O D R O H C S M C P H E O A
L O R E N Z H A R T W B O T S E R P R T
O T W Z Q N O T G N I L L E E K U D P S
G W U J Z N I W H S R E G A R I W Y M O
R S J N L O U I S A R M S T R O N G I G
E L B M E S N E U G U F O L K G E G R X
P O P E L B L H Q L F W M R R X F B T N
```

ALAN JAY LERNER

BAGPIPES

BATON

BENNY GOODMAN

BRAHMS

BRITTEN

CHIMES

CHORDOPHONE

CODA

CONGAS

CRESCENDO

DRUMMER

DUKE ELLINGTON

ENSEMBLE

FOLK

FUGUE

HOAGY CARMICHAEL

IMPROVISATION

IRA GERSHWIN

IRVING BERLIN

JOHNNY MERCER

LATIN JAZZ

LEONARD BERNSTEIN

LORENZ HART

LOUIS ARMSTRONG

MELODY

MILT JACKSON

PERFORMANCE

PERGOLESI

POP

PRESTO

SCARLATTI

SHOSTAKOVICH

SINGING

SKA

SMOOTH

STAN KENTON

STRINGS

TIMPANI

TUBA

TUNE

VIBRAPHONE

VOICE

Solution on page 152

Animal World

```
E L H W X F D G V I U N I R H E H G C F
L S P A R R O T C G J S O A Y E K N O M
J E I P V H F E X O F J W V Y Z T I I J
K L N O T M W K L D D K S E A L A M X P
H A T R T G D P H E A S A N T L E M A C
Q H A C A R M B G I L A M O N S T E R T
L W N U A O O W N R B Y R Q Y A O L H D
E I Q P N L E T M I C E D B S J P C I X
V T O I Z A E V F A U O A M O G Z N N F
S E S N S F W L V R S G A V W C L O O J
L L W E R F E S L P R N N P E A C O C K
H E L I E U W W T E I I F E I R F B E Z
Q N O S I B C B O A Z M P T P H F A R X
O Q T O A D E A N T E A T E R R S B O A
E L T F S P L D U P N L G P F U B P S M
P I E G S L E W L T J F A T W F O N G T
U K R R I V Q E H I T K N U K S A O O K
T R M R I J E E R W W R E T S O O R D G
A G O L G Z R A C C O O N U U Q W E I K
I G H W F W F T F E L O M N H T X H V G
```

ANTEATER

BABOON

BEAVER

BISON

BUFFALO

CAMEL

COBRA

DOGS

FLAMINGO

FOX

GAZELLE

GILA MONSTER

GIRAFFE

GORILLA

HAWK

HERON

LEMMING

LEOPARD

LION

MICE

MOLE

MONKEY

OPOSSUM

OTTER

PANTHER

PARROT

PEACOCK

PENGUIN

PHEASANT

PORCUPINE

PRAIRIE DOG

RACCOON

RAVEN

RHINOCEROS

ROOSTER

SEAL

SKUNK

SWAN

TASMANIAN DEVIL

TOAD

TORTOISE

WARTHOG

WEASEL

WHALE

WILDEBEEST

Solution on page 152

Going to College

YXSUPMACBUCUZEBMZTEI
RUELFTOSGNGUWMAJORPI
YVJIOSEGELLOCOOKTHVV
OITUTOKLUNIVERSITYPC
GRADSCHOOLELAYZRLALM
RNJSPKPCOTSEROFEKAWL
DEURWEAYSBEKDIAQFWGL
SNAOLTNEDUTSFGNUNGRE
TYPSYWRNVGAXUVBIONAN
URASSMBGSTUEEARRRINR
DOWETKAWETDTMTUETRTO
YTAFCATHFOAGTXTMHESC
IICOEXNHGGRTXSGEWEXD
NMARJLWFLIGGEIENENNI
GRDPBKLOOURWEBRTSIYP
VOEAUACTTREBSTSSTGNL
ADMISSIONSDJZHOIENYO
TLIBREDNAVNWORBWREGM
EHCETLACXAUVILLANOVA
NOITACUDEYRADNOCESBT

ACADEMIC
ADMISSIONS
AID
BRIGHAM YOUNG
BROWN
CALTECH
CAMPUS
CASE WESTERN
COLGATE
COLLEGES
CORNELL
COST
DIPLOMA
DORMITORY
EMORY
ENGINEERING
GEORGETOWN
GRAD SCHOOL
GRANTS
IVY LEAGUE
MAJOR
NORTHWESTERN
PENN STATE
PROFESSORS

REQUIREMENTS
RUTGERS
SAT
SCHOOLS
SECONDARY EDUCATION
STANFORD
STUDENT LOANS
STUDYING
SUBJECTS
TEST
TEXTBOOKS

UNDERGRADUATE
UNIVERSITY
VANDERBILT
VILLANOVA
WAKE FOREST
YALE

Solution on page 152

Book Nook

```
Y S D N E K O O B X D X I M V J R H Y H
W C C A C T I O N S L A N R U O J E S J
Y I A R M B P Z H M A G A Z I N E S B C
I S Y R E A D I N G C C C X F Q L G O D
O T S A M S B X S R I O P J E X O M O S
C O P T O R R E E H R H E L P D E S K M
N R I I I E O V S B O U N D J D N N M B
T I R V R T O A U T T R H L Y G M I A U
B E I E S C M P O V S R T E L S I A R O
S S T J D A S G N L I E E S U Z C G K T
K U U R R R R U C R H V L L T O K R I Y
X Z A D O A Z L N F R I M L L O H A N D
X H L O P H B G I A R E T L E I R B Y Z
H N L H X C N C H Y M W E F G R R Y R Q
C M S N O I T C I F E C N E I C S H E Y
Z U K K K I T E R U T A R E T I L P T Q
A L M O O E S L A I R O T I D E G G S O
Y O O N K E F F O O T N O T E S A H Y A
A C A S P M O N O G R A P H V O L U M E
U L B R W S H E L V E S E L Z Z U P N Q
```

ACTION

AISLE

BARGAINS

BESTSELLERS

BOOKENDS

BOOKMARK

BOUND

CHARACTERS

COLLECTION

COLUMN

COMEDY

COOKING

DRAMA

EDITORIAL

FICTIONAL

FOOTNOTES

HAND

HARDCOVER

HELP DESK

HISTORICAL

INDEX

JOURNALS

LITERATURE

MAGAZINES

MANUSCRIPT

MEMOIRS

MONOGRAPH

MYSTERY

NARRATIVE

PHOTOGRAPHS

PUZZLES

READING

REVIEW

SCIENCE FICTION

SHELVES

SHORT STORY

SKETCH

SPIRITUAL

STORIES

THRILLER

VOLUME

Solution on page 152

Free Lunch

AMBROSIA

ANCHOVIES

APPLESAUCE

BACON

BEAN SOUP

CABBAGE

CAESAR

CATSUP

CHILI PEPPER

CHINESE CHICKEN

CINNAMON

CLAM CHOWDER

COLD CUTS

COLE SLAW

CREAMY

CROUTONS

EGG SALAD

FALAFEL

GAZPACHO

GINGER

GUMBO

HOG DOG

JAM

MACARONI

```
W C L E F A L A F D K H L M D P C A G W
Y R E C G E D R R A S E A C R U H N N N
S E E N P A C A A E R J X W A O I C P F
E A K D I K B I L X P C R G T S N H M C
A M R R W R S B R A O P O W S N E O N Q
I Y I R U O A O A L S T E E U A S V O E
A C A B R T H M D C N G R P M E E I M C
R W T B E C A C B E C D G E I B C E A U
V N M G A P U P M U D A A A E S L H S N A
I A E P D T U I A A S T E G A P I F N S
N V Z K S S P O L E L S G C O C C H I E
E A M S T C C A S O S C N T A Q K A C L
G Q Y A H O S A A O C T A O L F E X M P
A J C Q H L M F R E T T U B T U N A E P
R T H R E E B E A N O A L O H U C E W A
B Q Z Z O S K V F S K G M Y R A O V P N
E M B I N L N H O G D O G O R P K R U O
Y E L S R A P U L G U M B O T K S P C C
D N S H M W P O R E G A N O O D L E S A
F Z N E B U E R E G N I G E M T U N T B
```

MEATLOAF

MUSTARD

NOODLES

NUTMEG

OPEN FACE

OREGANO

PARSLEY

PEANUT BUTTER

PIMENTO

POTATO SOUP

REUBEN

RICE

SALAD DRESSING

SESAME OIL

SPROUTS

SUBMARINE

THREE BEAN

TOMATO SOUP

TURKEY

VEGETABLES

VINEGAR

Solution on page 152

The Tube

```
H N K A H D G M C S S E T H X F A I P F
Y N N H I P I C T U R E T I L L E T A S
L J S W O D A H S K R A D S A H U D R W
E Y Q G C M T H E W E S T W I N G A E O
N L C O M E D Y C E N T R A L G S F M H
B Y R E V O C S I D M H T I S O E A A S
G S E T T E S S A C O E D I V L S M C K
U L H S S L A N G I S W M S K E A I L L
I O T N R I E S P N K O S T X N M L A A
D D O O O F E V O A R R D A K N E Y S T
I I R S T E B I C G O L N R S A S G E H
N N B T C T S U A N W D E G G H T U R M
G A G E A I Z V B V T T I U N C R Y D T
L C I J V M V O L H E U R R I L E E I P
I I B E S E I R E S N R F T T E E E S L
G R L H E L E C T R O N I C A V T R C D
H E B T D F I B T H E S O P R A N O S X
T M B O B T H E B U I L D E R R D C L N
N A C Z Y X V D L R O W R E H T O N A B
T H G I K X H V G S B U R C S S W E N D
```

ACTORS

AMERICAN IDOL

ANOTHER WORLD

AS THE WORLD TURNS

BBC

BIG BROTHER

BOB THE BUILDER

CABLE

CAMERA

COMEDY CENTRAL

DARK SHADOWS

DISCOVERY

ELECTRONIC

ENCORE

ESPN

FAMILY GUY

FRIENDS

GUIDING LIGHT

HDTV

LASERDISCS

LCD

LIFETIME

NETWORKS

NEWS

PICTURE

RATINGS

RUGRATS

SATELLITE

SCRUBS

SERIES

SESAME STREET

SEX AND THE CITY

SIGNALS

TALK SHOWS

TELEVISION SET

THE JETSONS

THE SOPRANOS

THE WEST WING

TRAVEL CHANNEL

VIDEO CASSETTES

Solution on page 153

Game On!

ARCADE

BASKETBALL

BINGO

BLACKJACK

BLOCKHEAD

BRIDGE

CANDY LAND

CAREERS

CATS CRADLE

CHINESE CHECKERS

CHUTES AND LADDERS

CRIBBAGE

CRICKET

DUCK DUCK GOOSE

EUCHRE

FIVE CARD DRAW

GUESS WHO

HEARTS

HOCKEY

HOPSCOTCH

JACKS

LOSE

MANCALA

MARBLES

MASTERMIND

MONOPOLY

PICTIONARY

POKER

RECREATION

SCRABBLE

SKILLS

SPORTS

STRATEGY

TIDDLYWINKS

TROUBLE

TWISTER

WIN

```
K F A V I O K T A X E E S I T W O C O S
D P I C T I O N A R Y S P K S T H H K X
P J A V E P M D D H K L O U O U W C V C
U R J S E L Z T D N I M R E T S A M T M
R F Q D C C R I C K E T T E S J S B U K
E E K C H X A S L L I K S E L B R A M L
T L C A I X C R K E V A U G T L O S E L
S B A R N I W G D G N G W X H O C K E Y
I B J E E D U C K D U C K G O O S E L R
W A K E S A K X L I R S Y G D N L T Z Y
T R C R E J T A L R L A N M N D Y B F E
M C A S C D D I V B E I W E A F E A Y E
H S L S H D A V O G B S U R L N X L M I
M T B T E R G H A N S C C N Y B C L V X
Q R A R C K V B X Q H S S G D P U A M N
X A S A K X B W I R T S M O N O P O L Y
N T D E E I L B E A Y C E C A K D I R A
Y E W H R B L O C K H E A D C E E W Q T
T G J C S K N I W Y L D D I T R Y S Z W
W Y L S K E U H C T O C S P O H N C L A
```

Solution on page 153

Right at Home

```
J D V Q P L P C R E H T A G B Q L X N O
C R E M M A H E A C U R T A I N S G C S
Q E U G R I A I K B K E T A E S E V O L
Z D K C M D Z L C L I H X N N R N F R C
J S P N I E S I P R R N M O O O A E Y A
C E E N V H M N H O R S E I I E D D R S
Z Y G G E B O G O R Q E M T W D L G I W
D S S L S E K M N R N V A A A E H U S O
T X F S R M E C E I V L T L L A W Y R D
V W H E X A D Z L M U E L I L Q S B I N
Y X T V E G E X I S R H I T P W S N A I
B S E O C A T P N H E S R N A S F P H W
H L L T A Z E I E A L K E E P E T L C W
M R I S L I C A S N A O P V E R O B G O
M O O C P N T N H D X O A P R U X Q N L
T C T L E E O O K T Z B P X S T H G I L
V E D E R S R E W O H S S A I C E W R I
F D U L I A S K K O Y A W E V I R D I P
R E J T F U P H O L S T E R Y P C J W I
X V S E L G N I H S S I N K X E X B T B
```

BATHROOM
BOOKSHELVES
CABINET
CEILING
CHAIRS
CHIMNEY
CURTAINS
DECOR
DRIVEWAY
DRYWALL
FIREPLACE
GATHER
HAMMER
HAND TOOLS
INSULATION
LADDER
LIGHTS
LOVESEAT
MAGAZINES
MIRROR
NEWSPAPER
PARLOR
PHONE LINES
PIANO

PICTURES
PILLOW
RADIO
READING
RELAX
SHELF
SHINGLES
SHOWER
SINK
SMOKE DETECTORS
SOFA

STEREO
STOVES
TOILET
UPHOLSTERY
VENTILATION
WALLPAPER
WATER HEATER
WINDOWS
WIRING

Solution on page 153

Get in the Car

ACCESS ROAD

BEARINGS

BEETLE

BODY WORK

CAR CLUB

CAR STEREO

CARAVAN

CARBURETOR

CHASSIS

CHRYSLER

CORVAIR

CREDIT CARDS

CROSSING GUARD

CUGNOT

DASHBOARD

DEFROSTER

IMPALA

JAGUAR

LICENSE PLATE

MECHANIC

MOTORCYCLES

PARKWAY

PERFORMANCE

PINTO

POLICE OFFICERS

POLLUTION

REGISTRATION

REST STOPS

SEAT BELT

SHOCK ABSORBER

SPORTS CARS

STARTER

STATION WAGON

STOP SIGN

SUSPENSION

THROTTLE

TRAFFIC

TRANSMISSION

VEHICLE

VW BUS

WHEELS

WIPER MOTOR

```
R I N S E L C Y C R O T O M C O S M I Q
Z P N E T T B X C G V R E T R A T S M G
U S Z A A Y U N O I S S I M S N A R T T
N I N T L A L O Z C N G I S P O T S M V
S S C B P W C R N O I T A R T S I G E R
U S H E E K R E B R O S B A K C O H S O
S A R L S R A C S T R O P S R F N L P T
P H Y T N A C U B O D Y W O R K W D O O
E C S A E P H G A C C E S S R O A D T M
N A L H C P I N T O L S H V R S G E S R
S R E C I F F O E C I L O P H R O T T E
I B R M L Y C T G N F V W B U S N C S P
O U B E A R I N G S J V O L E X A W E I
N R A U G A J G N A V A R A C R H H R W
B E E T L E U C Z Z R R E T S O R F E D
C T S D R A C T I D E R C T A L A P M I
Z O P E R F O R M A N C E L T T O R H T
B R T D K B O R I A V R O C I F F A R T
S L E E H W L Q N M E C H A N I C E V P
H O N O I T U L L O P E L C I H E V X H
```

Solution on page 153

Nine Lives

```
D W T S R E T A W U G E V U W V C W C E
X C K P N S F M H M G L A F K O D O K S
S X K R I E A W D G A M T M M V L T W U
I N M I L N T O M M N L I P O O N A U O
S E Y R X I T T M A V H A L R A L C U H
D L M S X L A A I W L N R P K C E I S E
T U E H P A M T C K I H O U B L X C B S
H J C E C B P A B O O I G O F A O O R E
G M I L P Y M J N O N A N G Q T T V T M
I X M T G V E S F T B C A J T N I C O R
F N W E Q X H A S F O E H I L E C X D U
K K D R R I A H T R O H S H S I T I R B
R S D E P K O C N E A H I E M R V L E N
O R E R P R U I S I F T K C N O L U T A
T E Z Y T E S E R O R J R W J A L F N E
A K B H E H N B L F K P U M A I P Y U P
D S A C R A A D C H A R T R E U X A H O
E I W E V L V X E R K R I K L E S L J R
R H X A L H E S E N I K N O T H U P X U
P W J S P P K L I T T E R B O X C O F E
```

BALINESE

BRITISH SHORTHAIR

CATNIP

CHARTREUX

CLAWS

COLORPOINT SHORTHAIR

COMPANIONSHIP

CORNISH REX

EGYPTIAN MAU

EUROPEAN BURMESE

EXOTIC

EYES

FIGHT

FUR

HAIRBALLS

HOUSE

HUNTER

INDEPENDENT

JAPANESE BOBTAIL

JAVANESE

KITTENS

LION

LITTER BOX

MAMMAL

MANX

MICE

MILK

OCICAT

ORIENTAL

PAWS

PLAYFUL

PREDATOR

PUMA

SCOTTISH FOLD

SELKIRK REX

SHELTER

SLEEP

TONKINESE

TURKISH ANGORA

WATER

WHISKERS

Solution on page 153

In the Ocean

```
O C A N A E N A R R E T I D E M C A I Z
G E D D O C E A N I C R I D G E L V Z T
R N R Z S B T T N D N H K M M D R I F T
T S I O L E E R E V E T M E N T T Q L S
I U A L H A D A A E I H A D U N E H I U
B R T H L S R I C N C N V O E S S C V N
A F I S E E K O M H S P K M I R E F E A
C I C U R D W C T E E P H G A B L O L M
K N T R U I A P A T N S O M E I A O O I
R G N P T T E L U B I T T R L P H D C S
U R B U A W E D P R R L G C T R W C I E
S O I R R V B S U B A S T A A A U H T A
H V O Y E L L O W S M A A N A Q T A Y M
G E S L P A N R E N I L N A E C O I Z O
N R P I M N K R E T S A E H T R O N O U
I W H N E K X W A T M O S P H E R E N N
H A E D T M E N A C I R R U H M R U E T
S S R I X N E A P T I D E F D P R A C S
I H E A D L A N D C E C O S Y S T E M G
F Y S N M O E N O Z F R U S T N E R A B
```

ADRIATIC

ATMOSPHERE

BACKRUSH

BACKSHORE

BARENTS

BEACHES

BIOSPHERE

BREAKWATER

CURRENT LITTORAL

DRIFT

DUNE

ECOSYSTEM

FISHING

FOOD CHAIN

HEADLAND

HURRICANE

ICEBERGS

INDIAN

MARINE SCIENCE

MEAN SEA LEVEL

MEDITERRANEAN

NEAP TIDE

NORTHEASTER

NOURISHMENT

OCEAN LINER

OCEANIC RIDGE

OVERWASH

REVETMENT

SALT MARSH

SCARP

SEA MOUNTS

SEDIMENT

SURF ZONE

SURFING

TEMPERATURE

TIDES

TRANSPORTATION

TSUNAMIS

UPRUSH

UPWELLING

VELOCITY ZONE

WHALES

YELLOW

Solution on page 153

Holding Court

```
D K T E E D H C N E B G F S C R E E N R
O C J O S F N S D A U A M P P I J F P E
L O D H N O C O N R D E M I T R E V O L
U L O V E D J K I E A S T N C M R U S L
O C U T F K S W A P N U R M D I S J T I
F T B H F H S W C V M I G O R C E S P M
L O L E O F A K I N G A Z V W H Y G Q E
A H E T I Y P L I I N T H E P A I N T I
C S D W A L K Q P A T R I C K E W I N G
I C R O S S O V E R D R I B B L E H H G
N O I T A L O I V E N A L V E J V I O E
H R B I V H L N K T O H S L U O F O O R
C E B M S S O K L A Y U P S M R G I K O
E B L E G I N C H E E R L E A D E R S O
T O E K B A C K B O A R D H N A Q E H D
E A R E V O N R U T J V B A S N T V O K
X R X E Q S I D E L I N E T N I F E T C
B D N P O O Y E L L A V J Y S A W R N A
O V X E K R E T E M I R E P N A A S Z B
P Q D R A W R O F G Y J E S N E F E D T
```

ALLEY OOP

BACKBOARD

BACKDOOR

BANK SHOT

BENCH

CHAMPION

CHEERLEADERS

CROSSOVER DRIBBLE

CUT

DEFENSE

DOUBLE DRIBBLE

FADEAWAY

FAKING

FANS

FAST BREAK

FORWARD

FOUL SHOT

GIVE AND GO

GUARD

HOOK SHOT

IN THE PAINT

JERSEY

LANE VIOLATION

LAYUPS

MICHAEL JORDAN

NET

NO LOOK PASS

OFFENSE

OVERTIME

PATRICK EWING

PERIMETER

POST

REGGIE MILLER

REVERSE

RUN

SCOREBOARD

SCREEN

SHOT CLOCK

SIDELINE

SPIN MOVE

SWISH

TECHNICAL FOUL

TIMEKEEPER

TURNOVER

WALK

Solution on page 154

Yummy Yummy

```
A O W E H W T B F E T R O T I A F R A P
D R T C T R I L E D U R T S G F T V A S
J E Y U E T M Y W Q L Z P I Z F R N T E
U P S A E Y D N A C N O T T O C C R I N
Z S T S J U J U B E P S P S O A A P N O
S I W O E M C Y X I E G Q C K T N D L C
A R Z O L R Q G L I M I O E Y O D J O S
S C G L L R T L F B I N S R M F I R Z S
T E Y T Y L O F O Q U G R E U F E P J C
D L C N B L A N T T N E L G G E D O V A
W P A I E T B M C J B R N N G E A P J N
C P R M A O F R H N A B D E N Z P C U D
I A A R N C E C A S Q R H Z I A P O F Y
C M M E S A T R F C R E U O W L L R R C
V X E P M I C E C R E A M L E G E N O A
F V L P A M Y X U X W D M K H C C B S N
G X I E N W M C H O T C H O C O L A T E
U E Z P M I N C E M E A T P I E T L I S
D A E R B T R O H S M K I S S E S L N T
G A I W H C T O C S R E T T U B M S G M
```

APPLE CRISP

BITES

BONBON

BUTTERSCOTCH

CANDIED APPLE

CANDY CANES

CARAMELIZE

CHEWING GUM

COCONUT CREAM PIE

COTTON CANDY

CRANBERRY TART

DESSERT

FROSTING

GINGERBREAD CAKE

GLAZE

HOT CHOCOLATE

ICE CREAM

JELLYBEANS

JUJUBE

KISSES

LEMON PIE

LOLLIPOPS

LOZENGE

MALT

MARSHMALLOWS

MINCEMEAT PIE

PANCAKES

PARFAIT

PEPPERMINT

POPCORN BALLS

SAUCE

SCONES

SHORTBREAD

SODA

SOFT

STRUDEL

TAFFIES

TOFFEE

TORTE

TREAT

Solution on page 154

Equestrian

```
W B N C U Z L C X S M W O L M Q S K S D
W X D C Z R J D N A L T E H S R X T E H
U D Z G F M J I U D F N O I L L A T S K
N I V X I L V B W D A R S Y J B S F G J
N C N W N S T Y O L S V I S L I Q A E C
H H Z A L R A K H E O F S E E L Z Z L O
Q G R V O F O N S A O T O N N N I U S Y
G E N T N G C H J J L F A R V D R F N F
V V J I I Q O C S M A M D R E S S A G E
A W M O D E M J P I P L A R T S I K H N
D W J G S E P Y L H P Z B G T B T H E C
N B G M R O E D O R A H N M A M M A L E
Q D O C M K T R W G G M A R E L S B D S
N V A N C L I E B U N N A U A E L R J R
Z J T O I A T P O C K I A N I B A O E U
I C J A T M I R L A C E D N B F Z W P Z
F N T E S R O H E C A R O I T H O N I J
C Y S E T H N L A H L P T N R P L A B F
Y G T U T H S T A K B A I G K R O W T Z
W X R P E E X Z A P S U B S O L P E I S
```

APPALOOSA

ARABIAN

BARN

BIT

BLACK

BREEDING

BROWN

COAT

COMPETITIONS

DRAFT

DRESSAGE

FARM

FENCES

FILLY

FOREST

GALLOP

HARNESS

HORSESHOES

JOCKEY

LEGS

MAMMAL

MANE

MARE

OATS

PALOMINO

PLOW

POLO

PONIES

POWER

RACEHORSE

REIN

RIDING

RODEO

RUNNING

SADDLE

SHETLAND

SHOW

STABLE

STALLION

TAIL

THOROUGHBRED

TROT

VET

WORK

Solution on page 154

CHAPTER 5

Mazes

These mazes will sharpen your visual-spatial intelligence. All shapes and sizes of mazes await you here. Some of them can be solved quickly, while others will demand more concentration. Every maze has just one answer. Here is a simple tip: when you come to a dead end, retrace your way back to where a path choice was made and take the alternative route. Using this technique you can make your way through any of these mazes.

Monolith

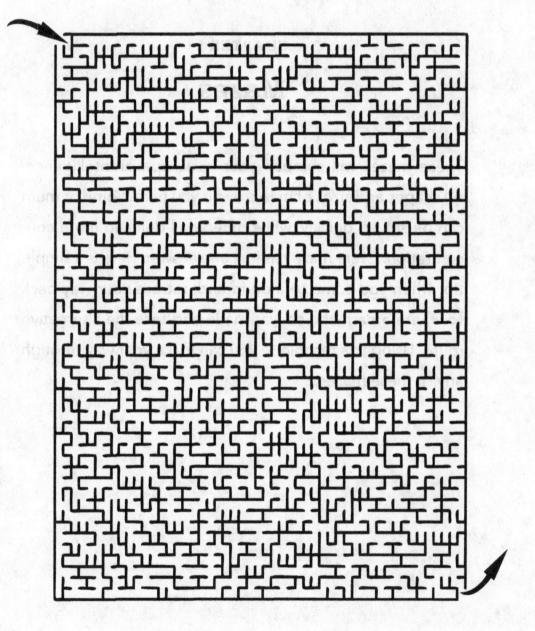

Solution on page 155

Inside Job

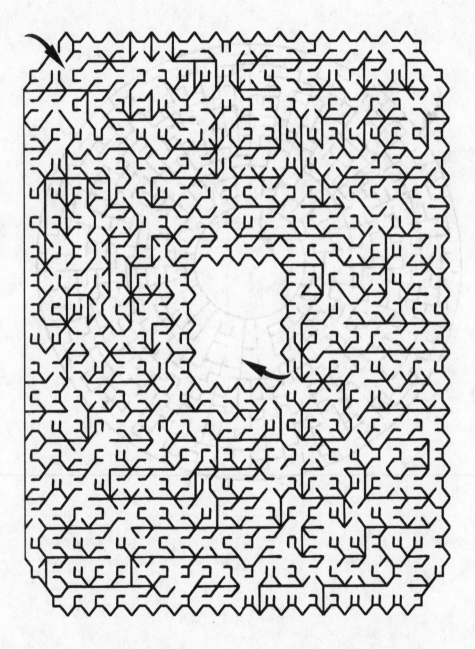

Solution on page 155

Doughnut

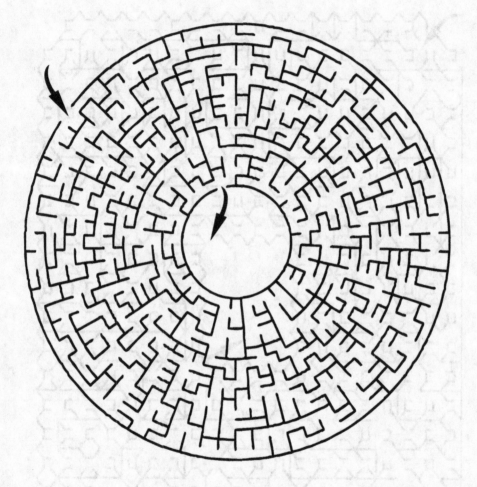

Solution on page 155

Going in Circles

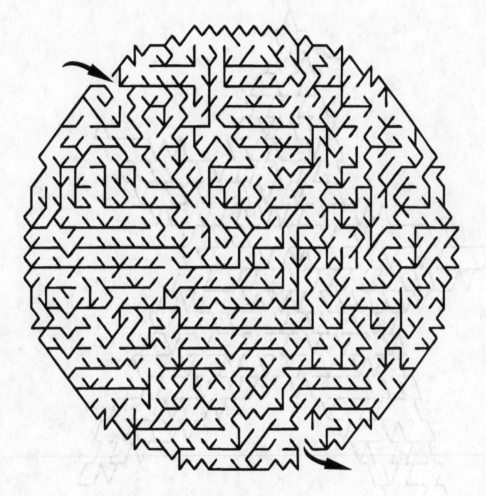

Solution on page 155

Starry

Solution on page 156

Round and Round

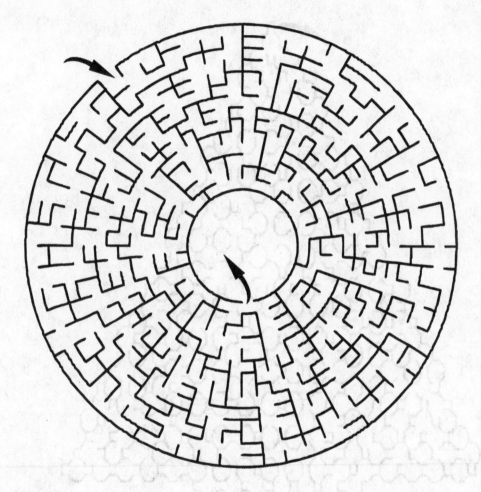

Solution on page 156

Arrow

Solution on page 156

Blocky

Solution on page 156

Hexed

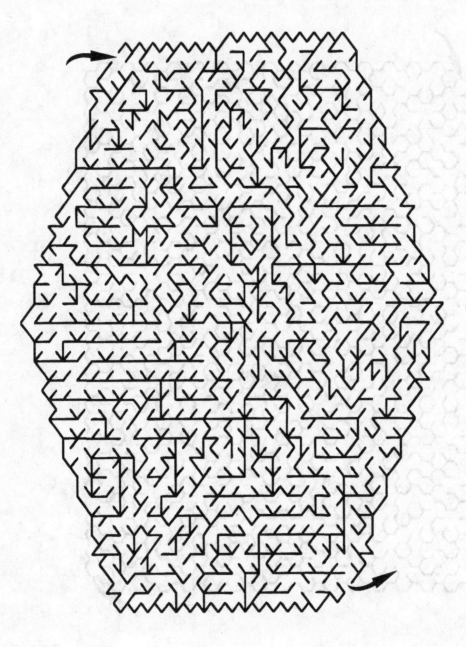

Solution on page 157

Egg

Solution on page 157

Pupil

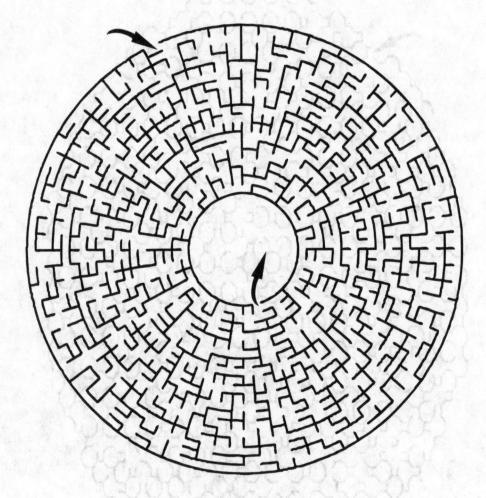

Solution on page 157

Disc

Solution on page 157

Right Angles

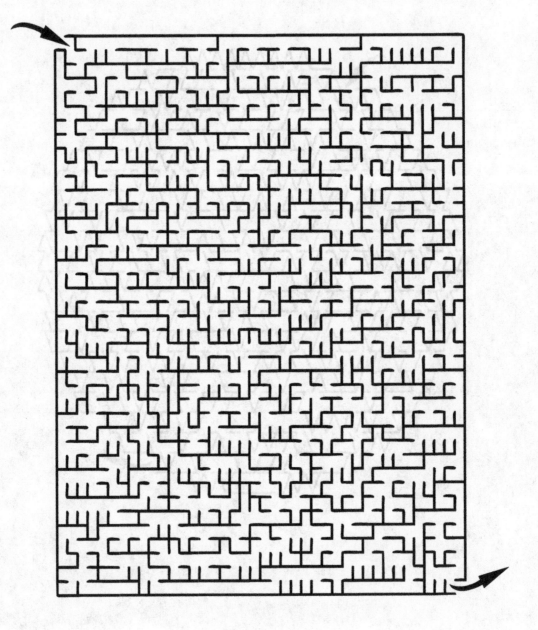

Solution on page 158

Curvy

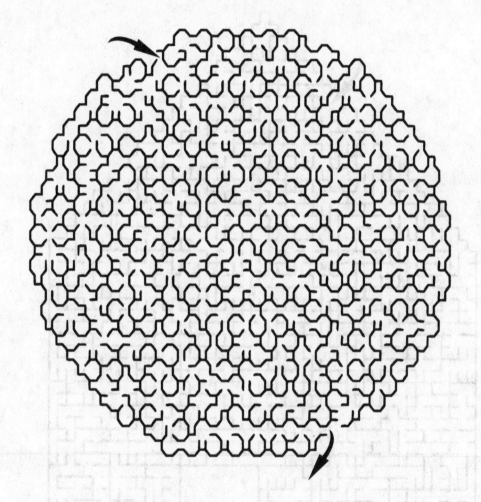

Solution on page 158

Going Home

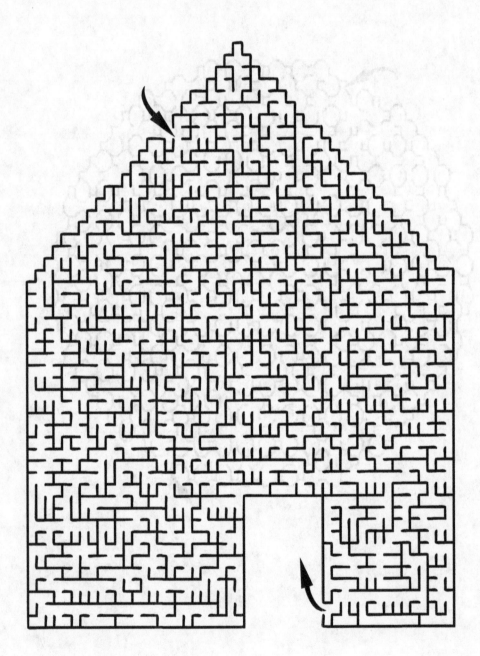

Solution on page 158

CHAPTER 6

Double Scrambles

Unscramble the letters to form words. Then unscramble the first letters of the words you made to form a word related to the title. Some groups of letters can be unscrambled in more than one way. For example, the letters ASEHC can be rearranged to form CHASE or ACHES. In these cases, part of the challenge is to determine the correct words so that the final answer can be formed using the first letters.

Example:

Breakfast Beverage	**The answer is:**
• NRABU _____	• **U**RBAN
• EJWEL _____	• **J**EWEL
• EXDIN _____	• **I**NDEX
• HREAT _____	• **E**ARTH
• AOCGR _____	• **C**ARGO
	JUICE _____

Not Napping

- APELP _____
- OKNNW _____
- ELAIN _____
- THEGI _____
- ETRWA _____

_____

Elevator Stop

- RXAEL _____
- AOSIS _____
- ISFTR _____
- ILGHT _____
- RFOEF _____

_____

Fuzzy Fruit

- ONPTI _____
- ACHKL _____
- PAYPH _____
- PETMY _____
- LATAS _____

_____

Lighter Alternative

- IILCV _____
- WLOTE _____
- ELHTO _____
- ERYCM _____
- AONNY _____

_____

Solutions on page 159

Salad Dressing Choice

- HDAER _____
- LOOCR _____
- IDARO _____
- EREVN _____
- ULADT _____

_____

Supersized

- EONJY _____
- EKLNA _____
- YALOL _____
- ELDIG _____
- ERACH _____

_____

Building Block

- ICBAS _____
- SIEAR _____
- MARKA _____
- ADINI _____
- AOCGR _____

_____

Earthling

- HYBBO _____
- MRALA _____
- NAUBR _____
- IHNTG _____
- MPEAL _____

_____

Solutions on pages 159–160

Log Home

- AINHC _____
- XINED _____
- ENAGT _____
- EBCHA _____
- NRHTO _____

_____

First-Anniversary Gift

- LTAER _____
- CPIAN _____
- AXTEC _____
- IRPDA _____
- RTYAP _____

_____

Breakfast Sizzler

- ANSAL _____
- CONEU _____
- BADER _____
- CRIAH _____
- LOALW _____

_____

Neck Warmer

- MECAL _____
- AORZR _____
- NAAGI _____
- RAIYF _____
- SEEPL _____

_____

Solutions on page 160

Concentrate

- CONEA _____
- LSIEM _____
- FTHIG _____
- LINTU _____
- ALANC _____

_____

Rodeo Rope

- NGARO _____
- SMPAT _____
- SONTE _____
- AMITD _____
- ELNAR _____

_____

Cow Chow

- UGGAE _____
- AYNIR _____
- AKENS _____
- SOONP _____
- ORCTA _____

_____

Halloween Choice

- RYPEL _____
- KYAKA _____
- ESEAT _____
- TCCAH _____
- IOTID _____

_____

Solutions on page 161

Light Lunch

- SELTE _____
- EEGAR _____
- OISDC _____
- EOLMN _____
- EUSMA _____

_____

Blue Casual Attire

- ESHPE _____
- EJUIC _____
- WBELO _____
- ANNNY _____
- EFTAR _____

_____

Goliath

- ONISY _____
- DUALO _____
- STTAY _____
- DERAG _____
- NPUIT _____

_____

Not Clear

- EIODV _____
- YNEME _____
- GVOLE _____
- SPEUT _____
- AGREU _____

_____

Solutions on pages 161–162

Power Source

- PAORE _____
- IREVR _____
- YEMBA _____
- ESATT _____
- LVEIO _____

_____

Chubby Checker's Dance

- EWLHE _____
- EHTNT _____
- OHRST _____
- LOIOG _____
- HCAET _____

_____

Soft Drink Size

- BUMHT _____
- DVLEO _____
- GEAMI _____
- YREMH _____
- BONYE _____

_____

Coffee Sweetener

- EUGST _____
- PLYPA _____
- RGTHI _____
- ESNEV _____
- ERCUL _____

_____

Solutions on page 162

Kind of Eclipse

- LVEEL _____
- OVABE _____
- OUNNI _____
- RDAYE _____
- SONIE _____

_____

Moola

- YAISD _____
- DEREL _____
- AAYRR _____
- EBCNH _____
- ARNVE _____

_____

Speeder Spotter

- AYDDD _____
- ARRWO _____
- GERID _____
- TAIOR _____
- TAPRA _____

_____

Golfer's Target

- LOYNN _____
- VNETE _____
- YSSAE _____
- RGDNI _____
- RAVIL _____

_____

Solutions on page 163

Cheesy Snack

- NYRAG _____
- OIBRT _____
- UHOGC _____
- FNIYT _____
- HYOEN _____

_____

Musical Toy

- ERODR _____
- IKKHA _____
- RBAOT _____
- EBZAR _____
- OUCRC _____

_____

Little One

- DCEYA _____
- ELDOG _____
- ICGRA _____
- HADNY _____
- SEUIS _____

_____

Drink Slowly

- TSART _____
- ILFRE _____
- EECNI _____
- RRERO _____
- CUTUN _____

_____

Solutions on pages 163–164

Unifying Idea

- HTEIF _____
- ECLTE _____
- ITXES _____
- NIORM _____
- LLOEH _____

_____

Place for Books

- BHAIT _____
- LGAEE _____
- YFNCA _____
- STMEA _____
- ALROB _____

_____

Close Encounter

- HCTHA _____
- USAUL _____
- GNERI _____
- LABGE _____
- SUCAE _____

_____

Gold or Silver

- ALWFU _____
- SRMAH _____
- TSNEE _____
- TLEAR _____
- EGPTY _____

_____

Sweetheart

- DMLAE _____
- GEALL _____
- GAONL _____
- EQALU _____
- TNOFR _____

_____

One of the Senses

- SEARE _____
- OMRYA _____
- ELESA _____
- DNUOS _____
- VLREE _____

_____

String Quartet Member

- JTEEC _____
- NROWE _____
- EGELD _____
- ECVAR _____
- ACLHT _____

_____

Elaborate Meal

- HETET _____
- AFRVO _____
- AOCNR _____
- YSTOR _____
- AXTER _____

_____

Solutions on page 165

Newsstand

- KKCNO _____
- URBCS _____
- NIKEF _____
- SEOEB _____
- IHSRI _____

_____

Problem for Jonah

- LERAS _____
- TBAOU _____
- GWEDE _____
- RTENE _____
- YDARH _____

_____

Full of Good Cheer

- EOMDL _____
- BTOOR _____
- YILDE _____
- OARST _____
- EALYR _____

_____

Pitchfork Wielder

- LAEEV _____
- RYNOI _____
- RVSEE _____
- TRYID _____
- ELEPO _____

_____

Solutions on pages 165–166

Symbol of Authority

- OLENA _____
- QEUPI _____
- EBGNI _____
- ODLLY _____
- GOESO _____

_____

Military Bigwigs

- IESZE _____
- RSBUT _____
- CETSN _____
- NGRAE _____
- RNOPA _____

_____

Supermarket Section

- LDAYE _____
- IRONB _____
- YNUOG _____
- GRNAE _____
- EALID _____

_____

Musical Speed

- MTREE _____
- NYNPE _____
- ENFOT _____
- NTGHI _____
- NETRY _____

_____

Solutions on page 166

Word Processing Command

- CERAT   _____
- NINRE   _____
- NOLEV   _____
- LPAEN   _____
- ATHNK   _____

  _____

School Group

- CTTIA   _____
- STUOC   _____
- DEAHS   _____
- RHCAT   _____
- ABLLE   _____

  _____

Quilt Square

- ONHRO   _____
- ALDPE   _____
- HRIET   _____
- ARRYC   _____
- AILEV   _____

  _____

Valentine Symbol

- IKTCH   _____
- EEFRR   _____
- AEENT   _____
- HGNIE   _____
- IELAK   _____

  _____

Solutions on page 167

CHAPTER 7

Cryptoquotes

In the following puzzles, each letter of the alphabet (A–Z) has been substituted with another letter. Your challenge is to break the code for each puzzle and decipher the quote and author. If you get stumped, there are hints for the puzzles at the end of this chapter.

Example:

U KLNV Q HLX. MV HLVA ZLCMUZX
OLJ RLKUCIQK JVQALZA.

—GUKK JLXVJA

The answer is:

I love a dog. He does nothing for political reasons.
—Will Rogers

Cryptoquote 1

YT VNS STG, ES EYXX QSCSCZSQ TIV VNS EIQGO

IB IHQ STSCYSO, ZHV VNS OYXSTPS IB IHQ

BQYSTGO.

—CRQVYT XHVNSQ JYTW FQ.

Cryptoquote 2

UDDYRLAF XIGF HYNH: U XIGF NIL JFPYLHF

U TFFS NIL. DYRLAF XIGF HYNH: U TFFS NIL

JFPYLHF U XIGF NIL.

—FAUPM KAIDD

Cryptoquote 3

U IVHUW SUGZ KHMKXH WPRGJ WPHZ UVH

WPRGJRGI TPHG WPHZ UVH SHVHXZ VHUVVUGIRGI

WPHRV KVHLQORNHF.

—TRXXRUS LUSHF

Solution on page 168

Cryptoquote 4

FUNI UX VC QI FUYIE, OCV JCOVWCFFIE, BOE

DRLBOUVG UX KCO QG JCOVUORUOZ VC TFBG UO

NBJI CN JIWVBUO EINIBV.

—WBFTD IFFUXCO

Cryptoquote 5

CVO VHGGAOMC SPSOQCM PX SI TAXO VHYO

NOOQ CVO XOK KVALV A VHYO GHMMOU HC VPSO

AQ CVO NPMPS PX SI XHSATI.

—CVPSHM BOXXOWMPQ

Cryptoquote 6

ZP LPG CPAAPM MSDFD GSD IVGS WVR ADVZ. JP

HLOGDVZ MSDFD GSDFD HO LP IVGS VLZ ADVKD

V GFVHA.

—FVAIS MVAZP DWDFOPL

Solution on page 168

Cryptoquote 7

AQ ECHU UPLC MPI ZHQF FSC PFSCE NCEYPQ'Y

WPPK. AQ EPTHQFAG UPLC MPI ZHQF FSC PFSCE

NCEYPQ.

—THEWHECF HQKCEYPQ

Cryptoquote 8

TQ HXBE ID XODQ TQJBZUQ OR HOLQU AIZ RMQ

JMBGJQ RI XILQ, RI YINC, RI FXBA, BGE RI XIIC

ZF BR RMQ URBNU.

—MQGNA LBG EACQ

Cryptoquote 9

JKS MKX'L QIL LK HAKKEI AKG JKS'TI QKPXQ LK

MPI. KT GAIX. JKS HUX KXFJ MIHPMI AKG JKS'TI

QKPXQ LK FPZI. XKG.

—RKUX WUIC

Solution on page 168

Cryptoquote 10

RNJY BIGRM HY NWJNWNUYRQ SDOONYF NJ BY

TIGRM IWRQ HY HIFW DU USY DLY IJ YNLSUQ

DWM LFDMGDRRQ DOOFIDTS YNLSUYYW.

—CDFP UBDNW

Cryptoquote 11

FICPEB AIBSAUSK PW O RSBPEEPEB. QSSNPEB

AIBSAUSK PW NKIBKSWW. ZIKQPEB AIBSAUSK PW

WXFFSWW.

—USEKG VIKH

Cryptoquote 12

GFP UF YBR RFP, UY'L FSY YBR DRGKL UF DSNK

XUMR YBGY WSNFY. UY'L YBR XUMR UF DSNK

DRGKL.

—GEKGBGO XUFWSXF

Solution on pages 168–169

Cryptoquote 13

MPZMRO PDMWD OHGDXUCVI XH ZCOU AHT;
HXUDTZCOD RHF ZCPP KD GCODTMKPD ATHG RHFT
WDTR UMSSCVDOO.

—KMPXMOMT ITMJCMV

Cryptoquote 14

NGHOECQ ND X CNL, X ZNNT EO X SXK'O ZQOH
DWEQKC. EKOECQ ND X CNL, EH EO HNN CXWT
HN WQXC.

—LWNGUFN SXWJ

Cryptoquote 15

UALCJWKM WU QDAF AYAJMKDWFH WU UAKKPAG.
QDAF FXKDWFH LEF DEVVAF KX MXC. UALCJWKM
WU KDA GAFWEP XN PWNA.

—HAJSEWFA HJAAJ

Solution on page 169

Cryptoquote 16

UX   MTAOT   JM   PYGGOOA,   RMYT   AOPUTO   ZMT

PYGGOPP   PIMYNA   FO   DTOHJOT   JIHX   RMYT   ZOHT

MZ   ZHUNYTO.

—FUNN   GMPFR

Cryptoquote 17

FLWJW   ZY   DAF   WDANTL   BGJEDWYY   ZD   GRR   FLW

XAJRB   FA   VNF   ANF   FLW   RZTLF   AS   WUWD   ADW

YOGRR   PGDBRW.

—JAHWJF   GRBWD

Cryptoquote 18

T   PGB'X   YZBX   ZBJ   JDF-EDB   ZCGVBP   ED.   T   YZBX

DQDCJHGPJ   XG   XDMM   ED   XID   XCVXI   DQDB   TL   TX

OGFXF   XIDE   XIDTC   SGHF.

—FZEVDM   AGMPYJB

Cryptoquote 19

XK BZZ ZVUK XVYL YLK FGNKMYVUK FT GKVHI
LBQQW; FDC ZVUKE BCK BZZ RVTTKCKHY BHR
WKY YLK EBJK.

—BHHK TCBHP

Cryptoquote 20

UAK ISBYH IK AZMK RBKZUKH DQ Z CBSHXRU ST
SXB UADPODPJ; DU RZPPSU GK RAZPJKH IDUASXU
RAZPJDPJ SXB UADPODPJ.

—ZYGKBU KDPQUKDP

Cryptoquote 21

DMXVRPRB FU XV VMR JRAVRB SG SKB NFGR
DFNN QR VMR USKBJR SG SKB URJKBFVL,
WKFOXAJR, DFUOST, XAO HSDRB.

—UVRHMRA JSPRL

Solution on pages 169–170

Cryptoquote 22

CV URNT FJ JFCZTB. FM FJ N ORCZTBMB
EYSBHJMNYSFYU RG MAB EYFKBHJB, XAV FM FJ
NJ FM FJ NYS XAV FM BWFJMJ NM NTT.

—JMBZABY ANXIFYU

Cryptoquote 23

KFJSJ BSJ PQOT KLP KSBMJEUJV UQ OUIJ: PQJ
UV QPK MJKKUQM LFBK PQJ LBQKV, BQE KFJ
PKFJS UV MJKKUQM UK.

—PVGBS LUOEJ

Cryptoquote 24

RAGV GZKLDWMQVM SWIV. SA RAGVFM, Z IAIVKS
JZK CV VSVFKWSO, VSVFKWSO JZK CV SQV SWJE
AY Z JRAJE.

—IZFO XZFFWMQ

Solution on page 170

Cryptoquote 25

LXLOKPUL GH D WLUGQH DI ALDHI PUEL D
KLDO. D OLDA WLUGQH BDH BGH POGWGUDA
GFLDH EAPHLO IPWLIBLO.

—WLPOW E. AGEBILURLOW

Cryptoquote 26

UOBF KFP HNJD EFYNQBF HAFG ANWF BCKFHAOPX
HC BNG; SCCJB, EFYNQBF HAFG ANWF HC BNG
BCKFHAOPX.

—ZJNHC

Cryptoquote 27

GRGDBJSRN WVEIT SO DSMZ HSOOZLCSRN G YTIN.
YZP QZIQDZ GTZ SRCZTZOCZH GRH CWZ YTIN
HSZO IY SC.

—Z.K. PWSCZ

Solution on page 170

Cryptoquote 28

AKO KBDKONA ZNO HU MRVBARC BN QHA AH
FRPO FHTO FHQOW, XZA AH FRPO FHQOW IH
FHTO UHT AKO XOAAOTFOQA HU CBUO.

—KOQTW UHTI

Cryptoquote 29

MLXU FLUJZ'W PCJW JAW WOUGU MABU V JWLZU;
AW OVJ WL NU IVFU, MABU NGUVF, GUIVFU VMM
WOU WAIU, IVFU ZUQ.

—CGJCMV B. MUKCAZ

Cryptoquote 30

MYBU MC WBQQ UYC ZCWOCU AX YBRRSLCZZ SZ
LA IAOC B ZCWOCU UYBL AVO MSQQSLTLCZZ UA
WYAAZC QSXC.

—QCA NVZWBTQSB

Solution on page 170

Cryptoquote 31

YN HYG JGMWZGFC WYN EZNCNMW, JGMWZGFC
WYN EKCW. YN HYG JGMWZGFC WYN EKCW,
JGMWZGFC WYN PQWQZN.

—LNGZLN GZHNFF

Cryptoquote 32

BDMBID KUML VGUMPKG DRBDUZDWJD ZC VGDA
XDDV IZCD GMWDYVIA QWE JMPUQKDMPYIA. VGZY
ZY GML JGQUQJVDU ZY OPZIV.

—DIDQWMU UMMYDTDIV

Cryptoquote 33

EW NFW CNAW EJBW IPO LG OKW FWDPZZWDOJPI
PS PYF QNBO, LYO LG OKW FWBQPIBJLJZJOG SPF
PYF SYOYFW.

—TWPFTW LWFINFA BKNE

Solution on page 171

Cryptoquote 34

XIMV RWT MZVB ZG GUBJC CTOZJN CR VZJE

GRPBCXZJN CR ER DZCX CXB CZPB DB XIHB

TWGXBE CXTRWNX MZVB CTOZJN CR GIHB.

—DZMM TRNBTG

Cryptoquote 35

WVS QXKB XJ XWJ PUK GRNYS, NKB XK XWJSRM,

YNK QNDS VSNHSK PM VSRR, NKB N VSRR PM

VSNHSK.

—EPVK QXRWPK

Cryptoquote 36

APXNET XEE VPA RXA DIXAK XKOPNDBIT, LQI BM

TGQ CXAI IG IPDI X VXA'D RUXNXRIPN, SBOP UBV

FGCPN.

—XLNXUXV EBARGEA

Solution on page 171

Cryptoquote 37

VZA OFECGVNWV VZOWJ OT WCV VC TVCE
KDATVOCWOWJ. YDGOCTOVH ZNT OVT CLW
GANTCW SCG AIOTVOWJ.

—NUMAGV AOWTVAOW

Cryptoquote 38

Z XHKK HK Z NVPQNI AWHGX EQKHSCQE TI
CZAOWQ AV KAVB KBQQGR JRQC JVWEK TQGVUQ
KOBQWLNOVOK.

—HCSWHE TQWSUZC

Cryptoquote 39

WPOE UNV BZZW QV YZ BQTMSSIAOS UAQN
PFHZTBAQE PTZ NPDDE; WPOE, PWAF STZPQ
PCCIMZOJZ, PTZ MQQZTIE WABZTPYIZ.

—QPJAQMB

Solution on page 171

Cryptoquote 40

ZJNYWF IBCX C QCG KRYZ IBYG BY LZ DCJPBX

RTT BLZ PJCNK LZ XBY UYZX YOLKYGDY CZ XR

IBCX ZRNX RT QCG BY LZ.

—D.Z. WYILZ

Cryptoquote 41

CRS NIX YRV FVSU XVC QSIF DVVF LVVOU RIU

XV IFJIXCIDS VJSQ CRS NIX YRV BIXXVC QSIF

CRSN.

—NIQO CYIHX

Cryptoquote 42

OXUXUKXO RSFFQCXNN EWXNC'Z EXFXCE DFWC

LRW VWD SOX WO LRSZ VWD RSTX; QZ EXFXCEN

NWIXIV WC LRSZ VWD ZRQCM.

—ESIX ASOCXHQX

Solution on pages 171–172

Cryptoquote 43

WNP ZFWWZP TODPEPEGPDPI RLWV CH MFOIOPVV
ROI ZCAP RDP WNP GPVW KRDWV CH R
KPDVCO'V ZFHP.

—QFZZFRE QCDIVQCDWN

Cryptoquote 44

GIF JFTFBW IFFJY UCIL GWVFXY, CIJ YG WVF
PVGEF VGQYF BY SQBEW BI WVF CBX CIJ UQYW
YGGI TGUF WG WVF NXGQIJ.

—SCEWCYCX NXCTBCI

Cryptoquote 45

VXCXJ AWJJZ DYWTU UKX ESMX WR ZWTJ
QKJSEUBDE UJXX. SV UKX XZXE WR QKSILJXV,
UKXZ DJX DII UKSJUZ RXXU UDII.

—IDJJZ ASILX

Solution on page 172

Hints

Cryptoquote 1: The word "silence" is found in the quote.

Cryptoquote 2: The word "mature" is found in the quote.

Cryptoquote 3: The word "people" is found in the quote.

Cryptoquote 4: The word "humanity" is found in the quote.

Cryptoquote 5: The word "moments" is found in the quote.

Cryptoquote 6: The word "instead" is found in the quote.

Cryptoquote 7: The word "romantic" is found in the quote.

Cryptoquote 8: The word "chance" is found in the quote.

Cryptoquote 9: The word "decide" is found in the quote.

Cryptoquote 10: The word "eighty" is found in the quote.

Cryptoquote 11: The word "progress" is found in the quote.

Cryptoquote 12: The word "count" is found in the quote.

Cryptoquote 13: The word "otherwise" is found in the quote.

Cryptoquote 14: The word "friend" is found in the quote.

Cryptoquote 15: The word "settled" is found in the quote.

Cryptoquote 16: The word "greater" is found in the quote.

Cryptoquote 17: The word "world" is found in the quote.

Cryptoquote 18: The word "everybody" is found in the quote.

Cryptoquote 19: The word "happy" is found in the quote.

Cryptoquote 20: The word "thinking" is found in the quote.

Cryptoquote 21: The word "wisdom" is found in the quote.

Cryptoquote 22: The word "universe" is found in the quote.

Cryptoquote 23: The word "tragedies" is found in the quote.

Cryptoquote 24: The word "clock" is found in the quote.

Cryptoquote 25: The word "original" is found in the quote.

Cryptoquote 26: The word "fools" is found in the quote.

Cryptoquote 27: The word "interested" is found in the quote.

Cryptoquote 28: The word "capital" is found in the quote.

Cryptoquote 29: The word "remade" is found in the quote.

Cryptoquote 30: The word "secret" is found in the quote.

Cryptoquote 31: The word "future" is found in the quote.

Cryptoquote 32: The word "honestly" is found in the quote.

Cryptoquote 33: The word "responsibility" is found in the quote.

Cryptoquote 34: The word "rushed" is found in the quote.

Cryptoquote 35: The word "place" is found in the quote.

Cryptoquote 36: The word "adversity" is found in the quote.

Cryptoquote 37: The word "curiosity" is found in the quote.

Cryptoquote 38: The word "lovely" is found in the quote.

Cryptoquote 39: The word "struggling" is found in the quote.

Cryptoquote 40: The word "evidence" is found in the quote.

Cryptoquote 41: The word "books" is found in the quote.

Cryptoquote 42: The word "solely" is found in the quote.

Cryptoquote 43: The word "kindness" is found in the quote.

Cryptoquote 44: The word "house" is found in the quote.

Cryptoquote 45: The word "children" is found in the quote.

CHAPTER 8

What's in a Name?

Find words using only the letters in a given name. Each letter in a name can be used only once in your word. For example, if the name is George Washington, then you could make the words *soar*, *grow*, *note*, and many others.

Robert Kennedy

Find 10 four-letter words:

1. _____
2. _____
3. _____
4. _____
5. _____
6. _____
7. _____
8. _____
9. _____
10. _____

Natalie Cole

Find 10 four-letter words:

1. _____
2. _____
3. _____
4. _____
5. _____
6. _____
7. _____
8. _____
9. _____
10. _____

Morgan Freeman

Find 10 four-letter words:

1. _____
2. _____
3. _____
4. _____
5. _____
6. _____
7. _____
8. _____
9. _____
10. _____

George Foreman

Find 10 four-letter words:

1. _____
2. _____
3. _____
4. _____
5. _____
6. _____
7. _____
8. _____
9. _____
10. _____

Solutions on page 173

Bonnie Raitt

Find 10 four-letter words:

1. _____
2. _____
3. _____
4. _____
5. _____
6. _____
7. _____
8. _____
9. _____
10. _____

Dave Brubeck

Find 10 four-letter words:

1. _____
2. _____
3. _____
4. _____
5. _____
6. _____
7. _____
8. _____
9. _____
10. _____

Sally Field

Find 10 four-letter words:

1. _____
2. _____
3. _____
4. _____
5. _____
6. _____
7. _____
8. _____
9. _____
10. _____

John Dillinger

Find 10 four-letter words:

1. _____
2. _____
3. _____
4. _____
5. _____
6. _____
7. _____
8. _____
9. _____
10. _____

Solutions on page 173

Charles Schulz

Find 10 four-letter words:

1. _____
2. _____
3. _____
4. _____
5. _____
6. _____
7. _____
8. _____
9. _____
10. _____

Kenny Loggins

Find 10 four-letter words:

1. _____
2. _____
3. _____
4. _____
5. _____
6. _____
7. _____
8. _____
9. _____
10. _____

Marlo Thomas

Find 10 four-letter words:

1. _____
2. _____
3. _____
4. _____
5. _____
6. _____
7. _____
8. _____
9. _____
10. _____

Steffi Graf

Find 10 four-letter words:

1. _____
2. _____
3. _____
4. _____
5. _____
6. _____
7. _____
8. _____
9. _____
10. _____

Solutions on page 174

Blaise Pascal

Find 10 four-letter words:

1. _____
2. _____
3. _____
4. _____
5. _____
6. _____
7. _____
8. _____
9. _____
10. _____

Zubin Mehta

Find 10 four-letter words:

1. _____
2. _____
3. _____
4. _____
5. _____
6. _____
7. _____
8. _____
9. _____
10. _____

Benny Goodman

Find 10 four-letter words:

1. _____
2. _____
3. _____
4. _____
5. _____
6. _____
7. _____
8. _____
9. _____
10. _____

Daniel Boone

Find 10 four-letter words:

1. _____
2. _____
3. _____
4. _____
5. _____
6. _____
7. _____
8. _____
9. _____
10. _____

Solutions on page 174

Tanya Tucker

Find 10 four-letter words:

1. _____
2. _____
3. _____
4. _____
5. _____
6. _____
7. _____
8. _____
9. _____
10. _____

Brigham Young

Find 10 four-letter words:

1. _____
2. _____
3. _____
4. _____
5. _____
6. _____
7. _____
8. _____
9. _____
10. _____

Walter Matthau

Find 10 four-letter words:

1. _____
2. _____
3. _____
4. _____
5. _____
6. _____
7. _____
8. _____
9. _____
10. _____

Desmond Tutu

Find 10 four-letter words:

1. _____
2. _____
3. _____
4. _____
5. _____
6. _____
7. _____
8. _____
9. _____
10. _____

Solutions on page 175

Guy Lombardo

Find 10 four-letter words:

1. _____
2. _____
3. _____
4. _____
5. _____
6. _____
7. _____
8. _____
9. _____
10. _____

Marvin Gaye

Find 10 four-letter words:

1. _____
2. _____
3. _____
4. _____
5. _____
6. _____
7. _____
8. _____
9. _____
10. _____

Loretta Lynn

Find 10 four-letter words:

1. _____
2. _____
3. _____
4. _____
5. _____
6. _____
7. _____
8. _____
9. _____
10. _____

Cheryl Tiegs

Find 10 four-letter words:

1. _____
2. _____
3. _____
4. _____
5. _____
6. _____
7. _____
8. _____
9. _____
10. _____

Solutions on page 175

Warren Beatty

Find 10 four-letter words:

1. _____
2. _____
3. _____
4. _____
5. _____
6. _____
7. _____
8. _____
9. _____
10. _____

Jasper Johns

Find 10 four-letter words:

1. _____
2. _____
3. _____
4. _____
5. _____
6. _____
7. _____
8. _____
9. _____
10. _____

George Harrison

Find 7 five-letter words:

1. _____
2. _____
3. _____
4. _____
5. _____
6. _____
7. _____

Alan Shepard

Find 7 five-letter words:

1. _____
2. _____
3. _____
4. _____
5. _____
6. _____
7. _____

Solutions on page 176

Calvin Coolidge

Find 7 five-letter words:

1. _____
2. _____
3. _____
4. _____
5. _____
6. _____
7. _____

Waylon Jennings

Find 7 five-letter words:

1. _____
2. _____
3. _____
4. _____
5. _____
6. _____
7. _____

Count Basie

Find 7 five-letter words:

1. _____
2. _____
3. _____
4. _____
5. _____
6. _____
7. _____

Smokey Robinson

Find 7 five-letter words:

1. _____
2. _____
3. _____
4. _____
5. _____
6. _____
7. _____

Solutions on page 176

George Lucas

Find 7 five-letter words:

1. _____
2. _____
3. _____
4. _____
5. _____
6. _____
7. _____

Humphrey Bogart

Find 7 five-letter words:

1. _____
2. _____
3. _____
4. _____
5. _____
6. _____
7. _____

Sigmund Freud

Find 7 five-letter words:

1. _____
2. _____
3. _____
4. _____
5. _____
6. _____
7. _____

Elizabeth Taylor

Find 7 five-letter words:

1. _____
2. _____
3. _____
4. _____
5. _____
6. _____
7. _____

Solutions on page 177

Marie Osmond

Find 7 five-letter words:

1. _____
2. _____
3. _____
4. _____
5. _____
6. _____
7. _____

Walter Payton

Find 7 five-letter words:

1. _____
2. _____
3. _____
4. _____
5. _____
6. _____
7. _____

Alexander Graham Bell

Find 7 five-letter words:

1. _____
2. _____
3. _____
4. _____
5. _____
6. _____
7. _____

Linda Ronstadt

Find 7 five-letter words:

1. _____
2. _____
3. _____
4. _____
5. _____
6. _____
7. _____

Solutions on page 177

Abigail Van Buren

Find 7 five-letter words:

1. _____
2. _____
3. _____
4. _____
5. _____
6. _____
7. _____

Neil Sedaka

Find 7 five-letter words:

1. _____
2. _____
3. _____
4. _____
5. _____
6. _____
7. _____

Ingrid Bergman

Find 7 five-letter words:

1. _____
2. _____
3. _____
4. _____
5. _____
6. _____
7. _____

Woody Guthrie

Find 7 five-letter words:

1. _____
2. _____
3. _____
4. _____
5. _____
6. _____
7. _____

Solutions on page 178

Aristotle

Find 7 five-letter words:

1. _____
2. _____
3. _____
4. _____
5. _____
6. _____
7. _____

Candice Bergen

Find 7 five-letter words:

1. _____
2. _____
3. _____
4. _____
5. _____
6. _____
7. _____

Dennis Hopper

Find 7 five-letter words:

1. _____
2. _____
3. _____
4. _____
5. _____
6. _____
7. _____

Richard Simmons

Find 7 five-letter words:

1. _____
2. _____
3. _____
4. _____
5. _____
6. _____
7. _____

Solutions on page 178

Howard Hughes

Find 7 five-letter words:

1. _____
2. _____
3. _____
4. _____
5. _____
6. _____
7. _____

Steven Seagal

Find 7 five-letter words:

1. _____
2. _____
3. _____
4. _____
5. _____
6. _____
7. _____

Rod Stewart

Find 7 five-letter words:

1. _____
2. _____
3. _____
4. _____
5. _____
6. _____
7. _____

Norman Rockwell

Find 7 five-letter words:

1. _____
2. _____
3. _____
4. _____
5. _____
6. _____
7. _____

Solutions on page 179

CHAPTER 9

Providers

Fit all of the words into the grids. To get you started, one of the words is already entered.

Provider 1

3 Letters

BEE
CUE
EAU
ERA
ESS
HAE
HOE
OAR
PAS
REP
ROC
SEE
SHH
TAO

4 Letters

ALAS
ALEE
ALES
ALTS
ANAS
ANTE
ARES
ARIA
BARB
COOL
COTE
DAPS
ERNE
EROS
GOLD

IRIS
LASE
LIRE
LOAN
LOOS
MAYO
NOTA
ORAD
ORLE
PART
PERT
REST
ROSE
RUSE
SLOE
STAR

TARP
TATE
TEAS
TOYS
URGE

5 Letters

ACMES
AROSE
BALLS
CATER
CEDES
COSTS
GATES

RIALS
SALSA
TENSE

6 Letters

LEARNT
NEARER
RESALE
SIESTA

8 Letters

PRESAGES
PROTESTS

Solution on page 180

Provider 2

3 Letters

AGE
ALA
ARE
ASS
CON
DIG
DUO
EON
HAP
HOT
NET
NIP
ORA
OXY
PAL
RIA
SAE
SAT
SEA
SOS
SPA
SRI
TAR
TEE
TOR

4 Letters

ADOS
ANES
ANNA
APED
APES
APOD
ASEA
BEET
CEES
CODA
KALE
LANE
LOOP
LOSE
LUXE
OAKS
OATS
ONES
ORES
PAGE
PALS
PHAT
PSST
SAPS
SARI
SASS
SECS
SEED
SEEP
SELL
SETT
SHAD
SLAG
SOLO
SORE
SOYS
SPAS
SPAT

5 Letters

ASSET
ENDED
ESSES
ESTER
SLATS
STABS
TAILS

Solution on page 180

Provider 3

3 Letters

AHA
ALP
ANE
ARC
ARM
ART
ASP
AXE
DIN
LET
LIE
LOO
LOP
MIX
MOA
OLE
PEA
POD
PUG
RIB
SAL
SHE
SOT

4 Letters

ALLS
AMPS
ANTA
AREA
ARIL
ARTS
ASPS

CEPE
CORE
DEMO
EAST
EELS
LAMA
LONE
MODE
OLIO
PENT
POLO
RIMS
RIOT
ROOT
ROUT
SADE

SCAT
SEAL
SHEA
SHIN
SLAT
SLOT
TAGS
TALL
TEAT
TELE
TODS

5 Letters

ALIAS
ASSES

ESTOP
PORTS
ROBLE
STETS
TESTA
TESTS
TSARS

6 Letters

LESSEE
SPARSE

Solution on page 180

Provider 4

3 Letters

AGO
AIL
ALE
ATT
BAA
DAM
DOE
EKE
HEM
HUT
LEA
LIS
OHS
ORE
OSE
PAN
PIU
POI
PSI
SAC
SET
SUM
TAN
TIC
UTA

4 Letters

ACME
AERO
AGUE
ALAE
ALOE
APER
ARBS
AWLS
BABA
BIKE
CENT
ETAS
HEAT
LABS
LAPS
LASS
MANO
MASH
MAST
OLDS
PARS
REES
RICE
SAME
SEER
SHMO
SOCK
SOLE
STOA
STOW
SUES
TAPS
TASS
TEED
TEES
TOME
TROT
TSKS

5 Letters

MARES
MATER
SCARS
START
TACET
TASTE
TORTS

Solution on page 180

Provider 5

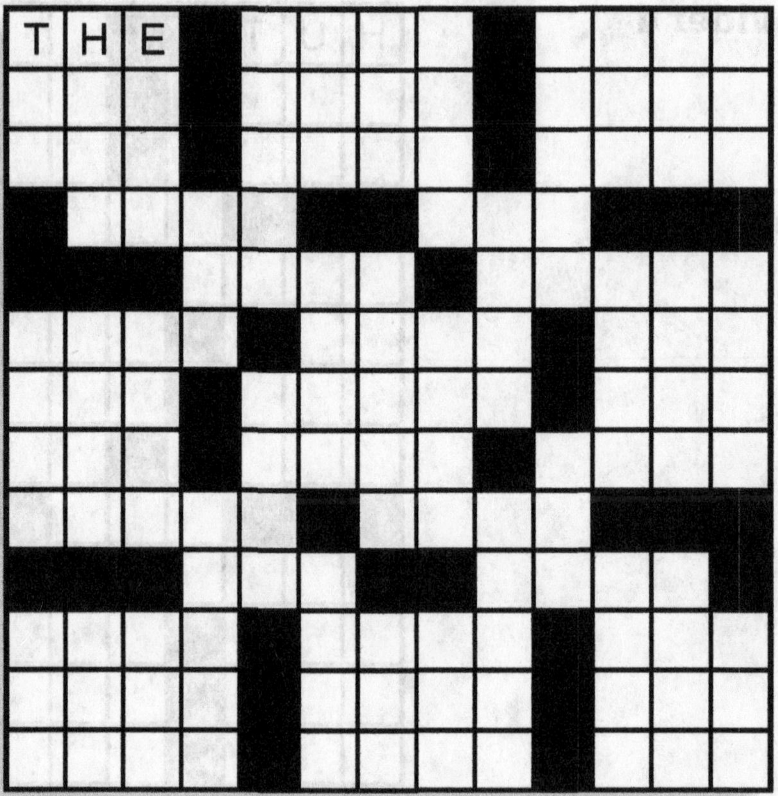

3 Letters

AGA
AIM
AIR
ALB
BAT
BEL
BEN
BOO
EEL
ELL
ENG
ERS
HON
ION
MAE
MOW
ONS
OWE
PAT
RAT
SOL
SUE
TAE
TEL
THE
WAR

4 Letters

ABBE
ALIT
AMAS
ANSA
ANTS
ARCS
AWAY
BEST
CHIA
DOGE
ELMS
ERGO
ETHS
EYES
FOES
FONT
GLEE
HAST
HATE
HINT
HOAR
LADS
LAIR
LOWE
MEAT
OSES
SERE
SHOP
SIRE
SLUE
SORA
STAT
SWAT
TONE
TOPE
TORO

5 Letters

GIROS
LASER
PEASE
RESET
SARIS
SETTS
SHALT
STAFF

Solution on page 180

Provider 6

3 Letters

ABS
ARK
AWL
BRR
ERE
ETH
HES
IRE
LAY
LIT
MAR
OCA
ODE
PAM
PIA
ROE
RUE
SIR
STY
TIE
TOE
TOT
TWA
WIT

4 Letters

ACHE
AILS
ALAN
ALTO
APSE
ARKS
ATOM
ATOP
BETS
BRIT
CHIN
COIL
ERRS
HALO
HONE
IMAM
LAME
LEAR
LOOT
MERE
NENE
OLES
PICA
RESH
SEAR
SEEM
SETA
SODA
SOME
TINE
TSAR
WIRE

5 Letters

ACRES
ALLEE
APSES
BEAST
CLASS
CRASS
ELATE
LATHE
METES
STARE

6 Letters

RETEAR
USABLE

Solution on page 180

Provider 7

3 Letters

ADS
ALT
AMP
ATE
AVE
BUN
COO
DAY
DOT
DRY
HAH
HOW
LAT
MAG
ONE
ORS
OUT
PRO
REG
SAP
TED
TWO
WEE

4 Letters

AGEE
ALBS
ARMS
AURA
AYES
BEEN
COME

DADO
DEED
EGGS
ELAN
ETNA
HELL
LODE
MALE
MATE
NEAT
OGEE
OUTS
OWES
POPS
ROPE
SABE

SANE
SCAD
SECT
SHAY
SHES
SOWS
STOP
STYE
TALE
TAUT
TEEN
THAT
THEE
TYNE
WOVE

5 Letters

AEDES
CASTS
LURES
PASTE
RESTS
SATES
SCREE
SENSE
STATE

Solution on page 181

Provider 8

3 Letters

AID
ANA
ANT
APE
BRO
ELK
ELS
ENS
EVE
HIS
LAS
LED
LEI
NAE
NOT
OHM
PAP
RID
SEN
TOM
TRY
WOO
YEA

4 Letters

ADDS
ALAR
ANON
AWES
AWOL
BALE
BENT
BRAG
CASE
CATS
EPEE
HOOT
ILKS
INNS
KINE
LAIN
LIEN
LION
LITE
MOTE
MYTH
NAVE
ODES
ORTS
OWNS
PERI
RIPE
SANS
SAYS
SEEN
SEMI
SKEE
SPED
TENS
TEST
TILE
TOES
TREE

5 Letters

ATLAS
BASER
BLAST
CASTE
GESTE
SLEET
SLICE
STEED
TEMPS

Solution on page 181

Provider 9

3 Letters

AMI
BAR
BOA
FEN
FIR
FLU
FOE
FRO
MID
NUN
OAF
ODD
OFF
OHO
ORC
PEE
PIT
SIN
SYN
TIS

4 Letters

AGIO
AGON
AMEN
AMIE
BREE
DATA
DEAN
EASE
EFFS
FLAP

FORE
HAMS
HART
HIDE
IDEM
LAMP
LIMA
MINI
OBOE
ORBS
ORCS
POST
RASP
SEAT
SHAH
SIDE

SLID
SNIT
STET
TAMP
TITI
TONS

5 Letters

BATON
DENSE
GIFTS
PLATS
RELIT
SNARE

6 Letters

AGREES
ARISES
ATONER
BERATE
FREELY
REASON

7 Letters

SORBETS
TASTIER

Solution on page 181

Provider 10

3 Letters

AWE
BIO
BRA
DAP
DEW
DEY
EAT
ERN
HUH
ILL
IMP
LEE
MUG
NUT
OAT
OBI
ORT
PAR
RIP
SAD
SHY
SOU
USE

4 Letters

AIRY
ALBA
AMAH
BOOB
COBB
CREW
EBBS
ECHO
ERAS
EWER
FEAR
FETA
ISMS
LADE
LARS
LOUT
LUGS
ODDS
OWLS
PFFT
PIPS
PLED
PREP
PYRE
RAIN
REAP
ROTO
SEES
SEWN
SHIP
SHOO
SLAP
SOAP
SPAR
SPOT
SPRY
TUBA
TYPE

5 Letters

BESTS
CHAOS
DRAPE
IDLES
PASSE
PASTS
POSTS
RIANT
SPENT

Solution on page 181

Provider 11

3 Letters

ALS
AMA
ANI
AVA
BET
ERR
FAN
FEY
GOO
HET
HUE
ICE
INK
LEG
MAN
NOW
OOH
OPS
PRY
RAW
REF
TEA
TEN

4 Letters

AAHS
ACES
ACRE
ARCO
AUNT
BIER
BRAT

BYES
CAPS
CHIS
EAVE
FLEE
GLUE
GNAT
ICES
LATE
LOGE
METE
NOSE
OARS
OFFS
PEAT
PEKE

PROA
RAFT
REAR
SALE
SEAS
SERF
SHOE
SONE
SPIN
SYNE
TART
TETS
TOOT
TWAS
TWIN

5 Letters

ANGST
BASSO
COLTS
EASES
NOTES
PUMAS
SABLE
STEAL
STENO

Solution on page 181

Provider 12

3 Letters

AFT
BOY
CAW
DID
EGO
EMS
ERG
GAM
GNU
HMM
LYE
NEE
PIE
RAN
REM
RES
RHO
RUM
TSK
UGH

4 Letters

ABLE
ACTS
AGAR
AGHA
ALOW
ARID
BERG
BURG
CITE
COON

FLAT
FOYS
ILIA
MATT
MIND
NORM
PURR
REAM
REPO
ROOM
SEEK
SLAW
SNOW
SNUG
SOIL
TAME

TEDS
TIRE
TIRO
TORA
TYES
WING

5 Letters

DWEEB
EDGES
MASTS
MELEE
RIFTS
TINEA

6 Letters

ARMADA
DROGUE
IRISES
MANAGE
PARADE
UNEASE

7 Letters

BARRIER
SEERESS

Solution on page 181

Provider 13

3 Letters

ABA
ABO
ACE
AND
ANY
BAD
BAL
BOD
BYE
DIE
EFT
GAR
HIE
KIN
LAD
NOS
OPE
OUR
PEN
PIG
RAY
SHA
SPY
YES

4 Letters

AEON
ANDS
ANIL
AVES
BABE
BAGS
BAKE
BEND
CARD
CUBE
DADS
DYNE
EDGE
FIAT
GIRT
HEAR
LENO
MOOR
OPTS
PETS
PILE
PRIG
PUPA
RENT
SAGA
SNAG
SPAN
TERN
TREY
UVEA
WHYS
YOGI

5 Letters

AGGIE
ETNAS
GREEN
OGLES
PESTS
RILLE
SLASH
STELE
TEMPT
WASPS

6 Letters

CHARGE
TEENSY

Solution on page 182

Provider 14

3 Letters

AYE
DEB
DYE
END
EWE
EYE
HAD
INS
MED
NAY
NEB
SKI
WAS
WAY

4 Letters

ABRI
ALMA
ANTI
BANE
BRAD
BRAE
CHAD
CLOD
DEAL
DEER
ELHI
EYRE
GROG
HERO
IDES

ILEA
IRED
IRKS
KANE
LAGS
LUNK
LYRE
MESH
NEON
OPES
PECS
PENS
RAND
RANT
REIN
ROMP

SLIP
SOLI
SOPS
STUD
WREN

5 Letters

ABBES
ARRAS
CODAS
CODES
DRAIN
HEEDS
MICAS

SEEDS
SEWED
SLOGS

6 Letters

COSTAR
GIGOLO
SEANCE
TIPTOE

8 Letters

EYEDROPS
WOODSMAN

Solution on page 182

Provider 15

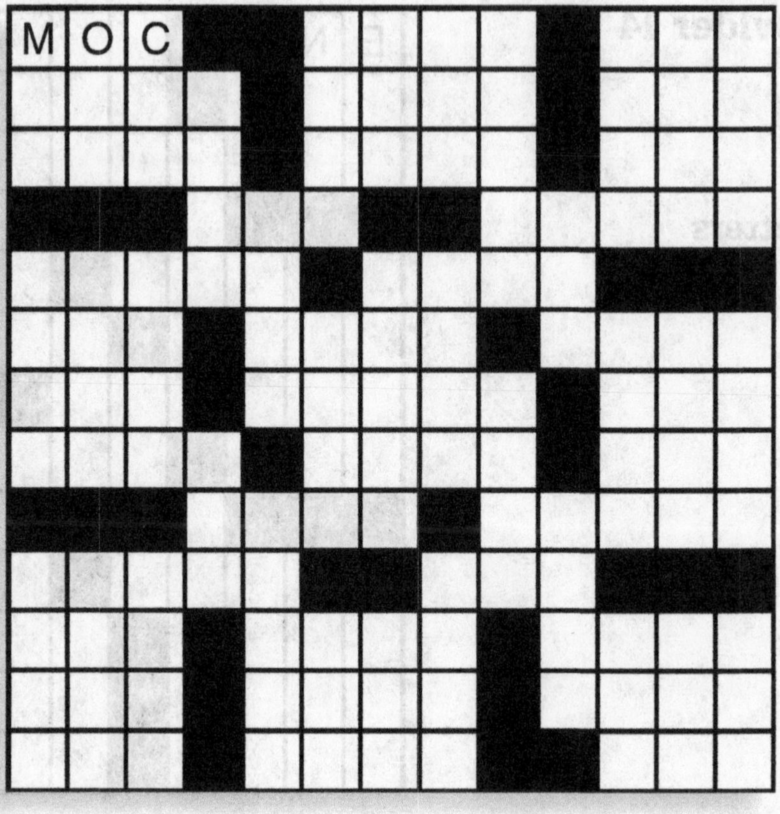

3 Letters

AAH
AAS
ARS
AWN
CEL
COW
DUE
DUI
ELM
GHI
GOA
HAM
HAS
ILK
IRK
MAS
MHO
MOC
NIL
ODS
OIL
OVA
REB
TAS
VIA
WHA

4 Letters

AIDE
ARFS
ASKS
AVOW
CLUE
COCA
COLA
DAWN
FLOE
GEES
HARE
HEEL
HIES
ISLE
LACE
OGRE
OLLA
OSSA
PAVE
RAIL
RAPS
SACS
SAGO
SAIL
SATE
SHED
SIBS
SKIT
SLED
TAMS
TANS
TWOS
USES
WHEE
WHIT
WRAP

5 Letters

CADET
COTES
GREET
SALES
SOLOS
SPACE
STOWS
TRIER

Solution on page 182

Answers

Chapter 2: Crossword Puzzles

Crossword Puzzle 1

Crossword Puzzle 2

Crossword Puzzle 3

Crossword Puzzle 4

Crossword Puzzle 5

Crossword Puzzle 6

Crossword Puzzle 7

Crossword Puzzle 8

Crossword Puzzle 9

Crossword Puzzle 10

Crossword Puzzle 11

Crossword Puzzle 12

Crossword Puzzle 13

Crossword Puzzle 14

Crossword Puzzle 15

Chapter 3: Sudoku Puzzles

Sudoku Puzzle 1

2	1	6	8	7	3	9	4	5
9	4	7	1	5	2	6	3	8
5	8	3	4	6	9	7	2	1
7	9	1	5	3	8	2	6	4
6	2	8	7	1	4	3	5	9
4	3	5	2	9	6	8	1	7
3	7	4	9	2	5	1	8	6
1	5	2	6	8	7	4	9	3
8	6	9	3	4	1	5	7	2

Sudoku Puzzle 2

6	2	8	4	1	9	5	7	3
4	1	5	6	7	3	2	9	8
3	7	9	5	2	8	4	1	6
5	4	7	9	3	6	8	2	1
9	8	1	2	4	7	6	3	5
2	6	3	1	8	5	7	4	9
7	9	6	3	5	2	1	8	4
1	3	2	8	6	4	9	5	7
8	5	4	7	9	1	3	6	2

Sudoku Puzzle 3

6	4	2	5	3	9	8	7	1
1	3	5	8	4	7	6	9	2
7	8	9	2	6	1	5	3	4
3	2	1	4	9	6	7	8	5
5	7	6	1	8	2	3	4	9
4	9	8	7	5	3	1	2	6
2	6	3	9	1	8	4	5	7
8	5	7	6	2	4	9	1	3
9	1	4	3	7	5	2	6	8

Sudoku Puzzle 4

3	7	4	9	8	1	2	6	5
6	1	5	7	2	4	9	3	8
9	2	8	3	6	5	4	1	7
1	3	2	8	4	9	7	5	6
4	5	9	6	1	7	8	2	3
7	8	6	5	3	2	1	9	4
8	4	3	2	9	6	5	7	1
5	9	1	4	7	3	6	8	2
2	6	7	1	5	8	3	4	9

Sudoku Puzzle 5

8	4	5	2	1	3	9	7	6
9	3	7	6	4	5	8	2	1
6	2	1	7	8	9	5	3	4
2	7	6	8	9	4	3	1	5
5	9	8	1	3	2	6	4	7
3	1	4	5	7	6	2	9	8
1	5	9	4	2	8	7	6	3
4	6	3	9	5	7	1	8	2
7	8	2	3	6	1	4	5	9

Sudoku Puzzle 6

6	5	9	2	3	1	7	4	8
7	8	2	4	9	6	1	3	5
4	1	3	5	8	7	6	2	9
5	9	7	8	6	2	4	1	3
8	3	6	1	4	5	2	9	7
2	4	1	3	7	9	5	8	6
1	7	8	6	2	3	9	5	4
9	2	4	7	5	8	3	6	1
3	6	5	9	1	4	8	7	2

Sudoku Puzzle 7

3	5	6	8	9	7	1	4	2
8	2	4	5	3	1	7	9	6
1	7	9	6	4	2	5	3	8
4	6	7	9	1	8	3	2	5
5	3	2	4	7	6	8	1	9
9	8	1	2	5	3	4	6	7
7	1	5	3	6	9	2	8	4
6	4	8	1	2	5	9	7	3
2	9	3	7	8	4	6	5	1

Sudoku Puzzle 8

8	5	3	9	7	4	6	2	1
1	2	9	5	3	6	4	8	7
4	7	6	8	2	1	5	9	3
2	8	4	1	6	9	3	7	5
6	9	5	7	8	3	2	1	4
7	3	1	4	5	2	9	6	8
9	1	8	2	4	5	7	3	6
5	6	2	3	1	7	8	4	9
3	4	7	6	9	8	1	5	2

Sudoku Puzzle 9

4	2	5	7	1	9	6	8	3
6	8	1	5	3	4	9	2	7
9	3	7	8	2	6	4	5	1
1	7	8	6	9	3	2	4	5
5	6	3	2	4	7	1	9	8
2	4	9	1	8	5	7	3	6
3	5	2	4	7	1	8	6	9
8	1	6	9	5	2	3	7	4
7	9	4	3	6	8	5	1	2

Sudoku Puzzle 10

8	3	9	4	2	1	7	5	6
6	2	7	5	8	3	4	1	9
1	5	4	7	6	9	8	2	3
5	4	1	3	9	7	2	6	8
2	9	3	8	5	6	1	4	7
7	8	6	1	4	2	9	3	5
9	6	8	2	3	4	5	7	1
3	1	2	9	7	5	6	8	4
4	7	5	6	1	8	3	9	2

Sudoku Puzzle 11

7	1	5	2	9	3	6	4	8
6	2	4	1	8	5	9	7	3
9	3	8	6	7	4	2	5	1
1	8	2	5	4	7	3	9	6
5	7	3	9	6	1	4	8	2
4	9	6	3	2	8	5	1	7
3	6	1	7	5	9	8	2	4
2	4	9	8	1	6	7	3	5
8	5	7	4	3	2	1	6	9

Sudoku Puzzle 12

3	1	6	7	4	8	5	2	9
8	4	9	5	2	3	6	7	1
2	5	7	6	1	9	3	4	8
5	8	2	3	9	1	7	6	4
1	7	4	2	6	5	9	8	3
9	6	3	4	8	7	1	5	2
7	3	8	1	5	4	2	9	6
6	9	1	8	7	2	4	3	5
4	2	5	9	3	6	8	1	7

Sudoku Puzzle 13

1	7	8	3	2	4	5	9	6
4	5	9	8	6	1	7	3	2
2	6	3	7	5	9	1	8	4
7	9	1	4	8	2	3	6	5
3	4	6	9	1	5	8	2	7
8	2	5	6	3	7	4	1	9
5	8	7	1	9	6	2	4	3
6	3	2	5	4	8	9	7	1
9	1	4	2	7	3	6	5	8

Sudoku Puzzle 14

8	9	4	1	3	7	5	2	6
2	5	7	9	4	6	3	1	8
1	6	3	5	2	8	7	9	4
5	2	1	8	7	4	6	3	9
3	8	9	6	1	5	2	4	7
7	4	6	2	9	3	8	5	1
9	1	5	7	6	2	4	8	3
4	7	8	3	5	1	9	6	2
6	3	2	4	8	9	1	7	5

Sudoku Puzzle 15

2	7	8	3	9	1	6	5	4
3	6	9	4	5	2	1	8	7
1	4	5	7	8	6	9	3	2
6	5	2	1	3	9	7	4	8
9	8	3	6	4	7	2	1	5
4	1	7	5	2	8	3	9	6
7	3	6	8	1	5	4	2	9
5	9	1	2	7	4	8	6	3
8	2	4	9	6	3	5	7	1

Sudoku Puzzle 16

4	5	8	3	2	7	9	6	1
3	2	1	4	9	6	8	7	5
6	9	7	1	5	8	2	3	4
7	3	2	5	6	1	4	9	8
5	4	6	8	3	9	7	1	2
8	1	9	7	4	2	6	5	3
9	7	5	2	1	4	3	8	6
1	8	4	6	7	3	5	2	9
2	6	3	9	8	5	1	4	7

Sudoku Puzzle 17

5	3	1	2	6	4	8	7	9
7	9	4	3	8	5	6	2	1
8	6	2	9	1	7	5	3	4
1	8	7	5	2	9	4	6	3
3	4	9	1	7	6	2	5	8
6	2	5	4	3	8	9	1	7
4	1	3	6	9	2	7	8	5
9	7	6	8	5	3	1	4	2
2	5	8	7	4	1	3	9	6

Sudoku Puzzle 18

8	2	5	7	9	4	3	1	6
6	1	3	5	8	2	9	4	7
9	4	7	1	3	6	8	5	2
5	3	2	4	6	8	1	7	9
7	9	4	3	1	5	2	6	8
1	6	8	9	2	7	5	3	4
3	7	1	8	4	9	6	2	5
2	5	9	6	7	1	4	8	3
4	8	6	2	5	3	7	9	1

Sudoku Puzzle 19

2	9	3	6	1	4	8	5	7
6	5	4	8	7	3	2	9	1
1	7	8	2	5	9	6	3	4
4	6	7	5	2	1	9	8	3
9	2	1	3	6	8	7	4	5
3	8	5	9	4	7	1	2	6
7	3	6	4	9	2	5	1	8
5	4	2	1	8	6	3	7	9
8	1	9	7	3	5	4	6	2

Sudoku Puzzle 20

4	3	9	7	6	5	2	1	8
5	8	1	9	2	4	3	6	7
6	7	2	8	1	3	5	4	9
9	1	5	4	8	6	7	2	3
7	4	3	2	5	1	8	9	6
2	6	8	3	7	9	1	5	4
3	2	4	1	9	7	6	8	5
8	9	6	5	3	2	4	7	1
1	5	7	6	4	8	9	3	2

Sudoku Puzzle 21

5	6	7	2	9	8	3	4	1
2	9	8	4	1	3	7	5	6
3	4	1	5	7	6	8	9	2
6	3	4	8	5	2	9	1	7
1	8	5	9	4	7	2	6	3
7	2	9	6	3	1	4	8	5
8	5	3	7	6	9	1	2	4
9	7	6	1	2	4	5	3	8
4	1	2	3	8	5	6	7	9

Sudoku Puzzle 22

1	5	2	6	4	3	7	9	8
3	7	4	9	8	1	5	6	2
9	6	8	2	7	5	3	1	4
8	9	7	5	1	2	6	4	3
4	3	1	8	9	6	2	7	5
6	2	5	7	3	4	9	8	1
5	8	3	1	6	9	4	2	7
7	4	6	3	2	8	1	5	9
2	1	9	4	5	7	8	3	6

Sudoku Puzzle 23

1	8	7	4	3	9	6	2	5
3	5	2	7	8	6	9	1	4
9	4	6	5	2	1	8	3	7
6	1	8	3	5	2	7	4	9
7	3	9	1	6	4	2	5	8
4	2	5	9	7	8	1	6	3
2	9	3	8	1	5	4	7	6
5	6	4	2	9	7	3	8	1
8	7	1	6	4	3	5	9	2

Sudoku Puzzle 24

9	8	7	2	4	1	6	5	3
2	6	1	9	3	5	7	4	8
4	3	5	7	8	6	2	1	9
7	5	2	3	6	4	9	8	1
6	1	8	5	2	9	3	7	4
3	9	4	8	1	7	5	6	2
1	4	3	6	5	2	8	9	7
8	7	6	4	9	3	1	2	5
5	2	9	1	7	8	4	3	6

Sudoku Puzzle 25

2	8	3	7	5	9	6	4	1
1	9	6	4	2	3	5	7	8
7	4	5	1	6	8	2	9	3
8	6	4	3	7	5	1	2	9
9	2	7	6	8	1	4	3	5
3	5	1	9	4	2	8	6	7
6	7	8	5	3	4	9	1	2
5	3	9	2	1	6	7	8	4
4	1	2	8	9	7	3	5	6

Sudoku Puzzle 26

9	3	1	7	4	2	5	8	6
5	8	4	9	3	6	2	1	7
7	6	2	1	8	5	3	9	4
8	1	9	6	7	3	4	2	5
3	4	5	8	2	1	7	6	9
2	7	6	4	5	9	8	3	1
1	5	3	2	9	7	6	4	8
6	2	8	5	1	4	9	7	3
4	9	7	3	6	8	1	5	2

Sudoku Puzzle 27

4	8	3	7	6	9	1	2	5
5	1	6	2	4	3	8	7	9
9	7	2	5	8	1	6	4	3
2	6	1	8	5	7	9	3	4
3	4	7	1	9	6	2	5	8
8	9	5	3	2	4	7	1	6
7	5	4	6	1	8	3	9	2
1	2	8	9	3	5	4	6	7
6	3	9	4	7	2	5	8	1

Sudoku Puzzle 28

2	8	7	3	9	4	1	6	5
4	6	5	1	2	8	7	9	3
1	9	3	5	6	7	2	4	8
7	2	8	9	5	1	4	3	6
5	1	6	2	4	3	8	7	9
3	4	9	7	8	6	5	1	2
8	7	1	6	3	2	9	5	4
6	5	2	4	1	9	3	8	7
9	3	4	8	7	5	6	2	1

Sudoku Puzzle 29

8	9	2	1	5	7	4	6	3
4	5	3	6	9	2	7	8	1
6	7	1	3	4	8	2	5	9
1	8	7	2	6	9	3	4	5
2	4	6	5	7	3	1	9	8
9	3	5	4	8	1	6	7	2
5	1	4	8	2	6	9	3	7
7	2	8	9	3	4	5	1	6
3	6	9	7	1	5	8	2	4

Sudoku Puzzle 30

1	3	9	5	6	2	7	4	8
8	5	6	3	7	4	9	1	2
4	7	2	9	8	1	6	3	5
6	4	3	2	9	8	5	7	1
7	9	8	1	5	6	4	2	3
2	1	5	7	4	3	8	9	6
3	6	4	8	1	9	2	5	7
5	8	1	4	2	7	3	6	9
9	2	7	6	3	5	1	8	4

Chapter 4: Word Search Puzzles

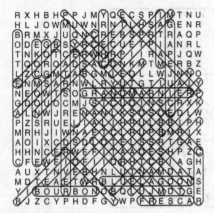

Drink Up

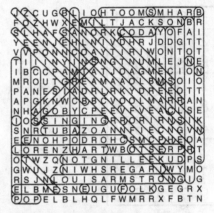

Beautiful Music

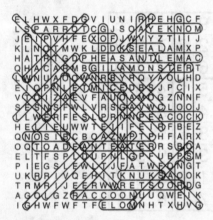

Animal World

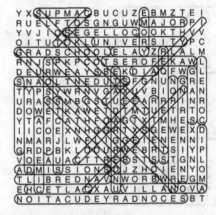

Going to College

Book Nook

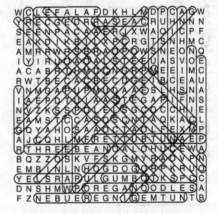

Free Lunch

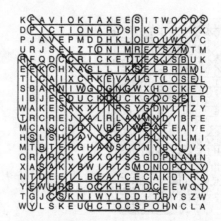

The Tube

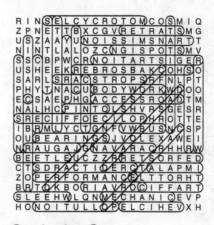

Game On!

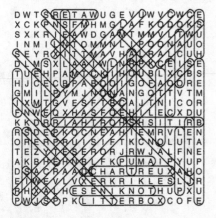

Right at Home

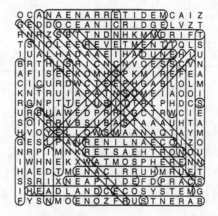

Get in the Car

Nine Lives

In the Ocean

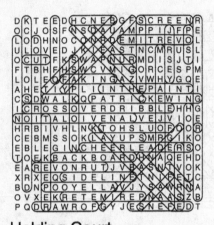

Holding Court

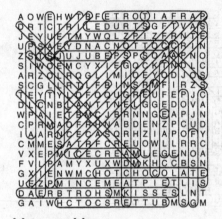

Yummy Yummy

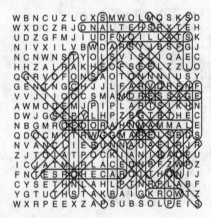

Equestrian

Chapter 5: Mazes

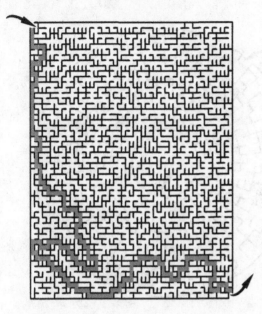

Monolith

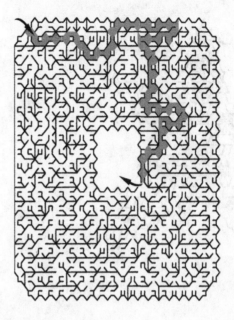

Inside Job

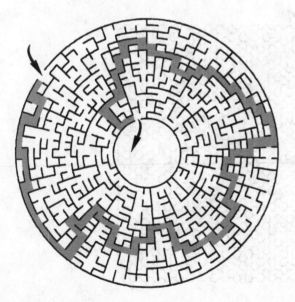

Doughnut

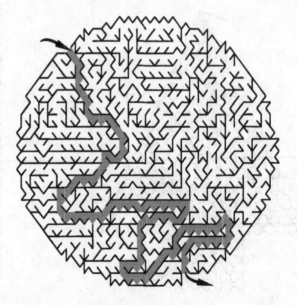

Going in Circles

Starry

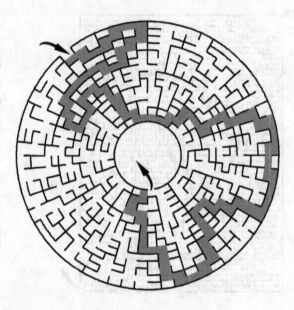

Round and Round

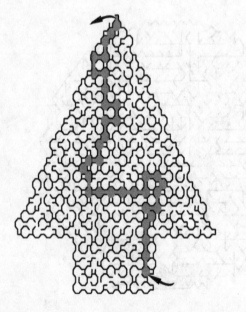

Arrow

Blocky

Hexed

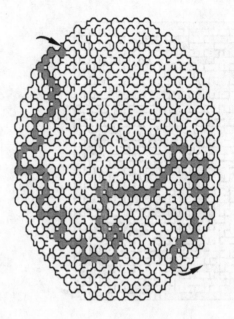

Egg

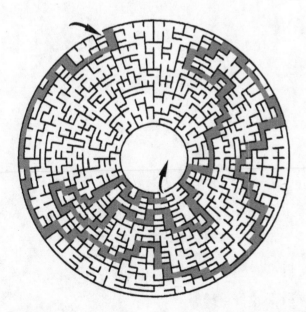

Pupil

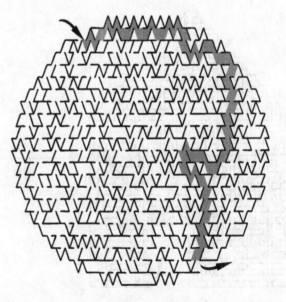

Disc

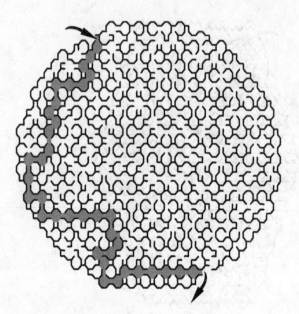

Right Angles

Curvy

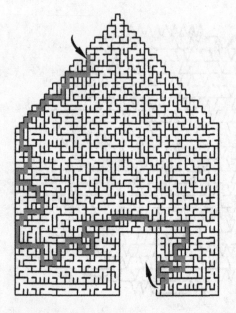

Going Home

Chapter 6: Double Scrambles

Not Napping

- **A**PPLE
- **K**NOWN
- **A**LIEN
- **E**IGHT
- **W**ATER
  AWAKE

Lighter Alternative

- **C**IVIL
- **T**OWEL
- **H**OTEL
- **M**ERCY
- **A**NNOY
  MATCH

Fuzzy Fruit

- **P**OINT
- **C**HALK
- **H**APPY
- **E**MPTY
- **A**TLAS
  PEACH

Salad Dressing Choice

- **H**EARD
- **C**OLOR
- **R**ADIO
- **N**EVER
- **A**DULT
  RANCH

Elevator Stop

- **R**ELAX
- **O**ASIS
- **F**IRST
- **L**IGHT
- **O**FFER
  FLOOR

Building Block

- **B**ASIC
- **R**AISE
- **K**ARMA
- **I**NDIA
- **C**ARGO
  BRICK

Supersized

- **E**NJOY
- **A**NKLE
- **L**OYAL
- **G**LIDE
- **R**EACH
- **LARGE**

Earthling

- **H**OBBY
- **A**LARM
- **U**RBAN
- **N**IGHT
- **M**APLE
- **HUMAN**

Log Home

- **C**HAIN
- **I**NDEX
- **A**GENT
- **B**EACH
- **N**ORTH
- **CABIN**

Breakfast Sizzler

- **N**ASAL
- **O**UNCE
- **B**EARD
- **C**HAIR
- **A**LLOW
- **BACON**

First-Anniversary Gift

- **A**LERT
- **P**ANIC
- **E**XACT
- **R**APID
- **P**ARTY
- **PAPER**

Neck Warmer

- **C**AMEL
- **R**AZOR
- **A**GAIN
- **F**AIRY
- **S**LEEP
- **SCARF**

Concentrate

- **O**CEAN
- **S**MILE
- **F**IGHT
- **U**NTIL
- **C**ANAL
- **FOCUS**

Cow Chow

- **G**AUGE
- **R**AINY
- **S**NAKE
- **S**POON
- **A**CTOR
- **GRASS**

Rodeo Rope

- **O**RGAN
- **S**TAMP
- **S**TONE
- **A**DMIT
- **L**EARN
- **LASSO**

Halloween Choice

- **R**EPLY
- **K**AYAK
- **T**EASE
- **C**ATCH
- **I**DIOT
- **TRICK**

Light Lunch

- **S**TEEL
- **A**GREE
- **D**ISCO
- **L**EMON
- **A**MUSE
- **SALAD**

Goliath

- **N**OISY
- **A**LOUD
- **T**ASTY
- **G**RADE
- **I**NPUT
- **GIANT**

Blue Casual Attire

- **S**HEEP
- **J**UICE
- **E**LBOW
- **N**ANNY
- **A**FTER

JEANS

Soft Drink Size

- **T**HUMB
- **L**OVED
- **I**MAGE
- **R**HYME
- **E**BONY

LITER

Not Clear

- **V**IDEO
- **E**NEMY
- **G**LOVE
- **U**PSET
- **A**RGUE

VAGUE

Chubby Checker's Dance

- **W**HEEL
- **T**ENTH
- **S**HORT
- **I**GLOO
- **T**EACH

TWIST

Power Source

- **O**PERA
- **R**IVER
- **M**AYBE
- **T**ASTE
- **O**LIVE

MOTOR

Coffee Sweetener

- **G**UEST
- **A**PPLY
- **R**IGHT
- **S**EVEN
- **U**LCER

SUGAR

Kind of Eclipse

- **L**EVEL
- **A**BOVE
- **U**NION
- **R**EADY
- **N**OISE

  LUNAR

Speeder Spotter

- **D**ADDY
- **A**RROW
- **R**IDGE
- **R**ATIO
- **A**PART

  RADAR

Moola

- **D**AISY
- **E**LDER
- **A**RRAY
- **B**ENCH
- **R**AVEN

  BREAD

Golfer's Target

- **N**YLON
- **E**VENT
- **E**SSAY
- **G**RIND
- **R**IVAL

  GREEN

Cheesy Snack

- **A**NGRY
- **O**RBIT
- **C**OUGH
- **N**IFTY
- **H**ONEY

  NACHO

Little One

- **D**ECAY
- **L**ODGE
- **C**IGAR
- **H**ANDY
- **I**SSUE

  CHILD

Musical Toy

- **O**RDER
- **K**HAKI
- **A**BORT
- **Z**EBRA
- **O**CCUR

KAZOO

Close Encounter

- **H**ATCH
- **U**SUAL
- **R**EIGN
- **B**AGEL
- **S**AUCE

BRUSH

Drink Slowly

- **S**TART
- **R**IFLE
- **N**IECE
- **E**RROR
- **U**NCUT

NURSE

Place for Books

- **H**ABIT
- **E**AGLE
- **F**ANCY
- **S**TEAM
- **L**ABOR

SHELF

Unifying Idea

- **T**HIEF
- **E**LECT
- **E**XIST
- **M**INOR
- **H**ELLO

THEME

Gold or Silver

- **A**WFUL
- **M**ARSH
- **T**ENSE
- **L**ATER
- **E**GYPT

METAL

Sweetheart

- **M**EDAL
- **L**EGAL
- **A**LONG
- **E**QUAL
- **F**RONT
- **FLAME**

Elaborate Meal

- **T**EETH
- **F**AVOR
- **A**CORN
- **S**TORY
- **E**XTRA
- **FEAST**

String Quartet Member

- **E**JECT
- **O**WNER
- **L**EDGE
- **C**ARVE
- **L**ATCH
- **CELLO**

Newsstand

- **K**NOCK
- **S**CRUB
- **K**NIFE
- **O**BESE
- **I**RISH
- **KIOSK**

One of the Senses

- **E**RASE
- **M**AYOR
- **L**EASE
- **S**OUND
- **L**EVER
- **SMELL**

Full of Good Cheer

- **M**ODEL
- **R**OBOT
- **Y**IELD
- **R**OAST
- **E**ARLY
- **MERRY**

Problem for Jonah

- **L**ASER
- **A**BOUT
- **W**EDGE
- **E**NTER
- **H**ARDY

WHALE

Supermarket Section

- **D**ELAY
- **R**OBIN
- **Y**OUNG
- **A**NGER
- **I**DEAL

DAIRY

Pitchfork Wielder

- **L**EAVE
- **I**RONY
- **V**ERSE
- **D**IRTY
- **E**LOPE

DEVIL

Military Bigwigs

- **S**EIZE
- **B**URST
- **S**CENT
- **R**ANGE
- **A**PRON

BRASS

Symbol of Authority

- **A**LONE
- **E**QUIP
- **B**EGIN
- **D**OLLY
- **G**OOSE

BADGE

Musical Speed

- **M**ETER
- **P**ENNY
- **O**FTEN
- **T**HING
- **E**NTRY

TEMPO

Word Processing Command

- **R**EACT
- **I**NNER
- **N**OVEL
- **P**ANEL
- **T**HANK

PRINT

School Group

- **A**TTIC
- **S**COUT
- **S**HADE
- **C**HART
- **L**ABEL

CLASS

Quilt Square

- **H**ONOR
- **P**EDAL
- **T**HEIR
- **C**ARRY
- **A**LIVE

PATCH

Valentine Symbol

- **T**HICK
- **R**EFER
- **E**ATEN
- **H**INGE
- **A**LIKE

HEART

Chapter 7: Cryptoquotes

Cryptoquote 1

In the End, we will remember not the words of our enemies, but the silence of our friends.

—*Martin Luther King Jr.*

Cryptoquote 2

Immature love says: I love you because I need you. Mature love says: I need you because I love you.

—*Erich Fromm*

Cryptoquote 3

A great many people think they are thinking when they are merely rearranging their prejudices.

—*William James*

Cryptoquote 4

Life is to be lived, not controlled, and humanity is won by continuing to play in face of certain defeat.

—*Ralph Ellison*

Cryptoquote 5

The happiest moments of my life have been the few which I have passed at home in the bosom of my family.

—*Thomas Jefferson*

Cryptoquote 6

Do not follow where the path may lead. Go instead where there is no path and leave a trail.

—*Ralph Waldo Emerson*

Cryptoquote 7

In real love you want the other person's good. In romantic love you want the other person.

—*Margaret Anderson*

Cryptoquote 8

Be glad of life because it gives you the chance to love, to work, to play, and to look up at the stars.

—*Henry Van Dyke*

Cryptoquote 9

You don't get to choose how you're going to die. Or when. You can only decide how you're going to live. Now.

—*Joan Baez*

Cryptoquote 10

Life would be infinitely happier if we could only be born at the age of eighty and gradually approach eighteen.

—*Mark Twain*

Cryptoquote 11

Coming together is a beginning. Keeping together is progress. Working together is success.

—*Henry Ford*

Cryptoquote 12

And in the end, it's not the years in your life that count. It's the life in your years.

—*Abraham Lincoln*

Cryptoquote 13

Always leave something to wish for; otherwise you will be miserable from your very happiness.

—*Baltasar Gracian*

Cryptoquote 14

Outside of a dog, a book is a man's best friend. Inside of a dog, it is too dark to read.

—*Groucho Marx*

Cryptoquote 15

Security is when everything is settled. When nothing can happen to you. Security is the denial of life.

—*Germaine Greer*

Cryptoquote 16

In order to succeed, your desire for success should be greater than your fear of failure.

—*Bill Cosby*

Cryptoquote 17

There is not enough darkness in all the world to put out the light of even one small candle.

—*Robert Alden*

Cryptoquote 18

I don't want any yes-men around me. I want everybody to tell me the truth even if it costs them their jobs.

—*Samuel Goldwyn*

Cryptoquote 19

We all live with the objective of being happy; our lives are all different and yet the same.

—*Anne Frank*

Cryptoquote 20

The world we have created is a product of our thinking; it cannot be changed without changing our thinking.

—*Albert Einstein*

Cryptoquote 21

Whatever is at the center of our life will be the source of our security, guidance, wisdom, and power.

—Stephen Covey

Cryptoquote 22

My goal is simple. It is a complete understanding of the universe, why it is as it is and why it exists at all.

—Stephen Hawking

Cryptoquote 23

There are only two tragedies in life: one is not getting what one wants, and the other is getting it.

—Oscar Wilde

Cryptoquote 24

Love vanquishes time. To lovers, a moment can be eternity, eternity can be the tick of a clock.

—Mary Parrish

Cryptoquote 25

Everyone is a genius at least once a year. A real genius has his original ideas closer together.

—Georg C. Lichtenberg

Cryptoquote 26

Wise men talk because they have something to say; fools, because they have to say something.

—Plato

Cryptoquote 27

Analyzing humor is like dissecting a frog. Few people are interested and the frog dies of it.

—E.B. White

Cryptoquote 28

The highest use of capital is not to make more money, but to make money do more for the betterment of life.

—Henry Ford

Cryptoquote 29

Love doesn't just sit there like a stone; it has to be made, like bread, remade all the time, made new.

—Ursula K. LeGuin

Cryptoquote 30

What we call the secret of happiness is no more a secret than our willingness to choose life.

—Leo Buscaglia

Cryptoquote 31

He who controls the present, controls the past. He who controls the past, controls the future.

—George Orwell

Cryptoquote 32

People grow through experience if they meet life honestly and courageously. This is how character is built.

—Eleanor Roosevelt

Cryptoquote 33

We are made wise not by the recollection of our past, but by the responsibility for our future.

—George Bernard Shaw

Cryptoquote 34

Half our life is spent trying to find something to do with the time we have rushed through life trying to save.

—Will Rogers

Cryptoquote 35

The mind is its own place, and in itself, can make heaven of Hell, and a hell of Heaven.

—John Milton

Cryptoquote 36

Nearly all men can stand adversity, but if you want to test a man's character, give him power.

—Abraham Lincoln

Cryptoquote 37

The important thing is not to stop questioning. Curiosity has its own reason for existing.

—Albert Einstein

Cryptoquote 38

A kiss is a lovely trick designed by nature to stop speech when words become superfluous.

—Ingrid Bergman

Cryptoquote 39

Many who seem to be struggling with adversity are happy; many, amid great affluence, are utterly miserable.

—Tacitus

Cryptoquote 40

Surely what a man does when he is caught off his guard is the best evidence as to what sort of man he is.

—C.S. Lewis

Cryptoquote 41

The man who does not read good books has no advantage over the man who cannot read them.

—Mark Twain

Cryptoquote 42

Remember happiness doesn't depend upon who you are or what you have; it depends solely on what you think.

—Dale Carnegie

Cryptoquote 43

The little unremembered acts of kindness and love are the best parts of a person's life.

—William Wordsworth

Cryptoquote 44

One deceit needs many others, and so the whole house is built in the air and must soon come to the ground.

—Baltasar Gracian

Cryptoquote 45

Never worry about the size of your Christmas tree. In the eyes of children, they are all thirty feet tall.

—Larry Wilde

Chapter 8: What's in a Name?

Here are some common answers; you might have found others.

Robert Kennedy

been, beer, bend, bent, body, bond, bone, bony, bore, born, debt, deer, deny, done, eyed, keen, knee, knob, knot, need, none, note, obey, reed, rent, robe, tend, tone, tore, torn, tree

Morgan Freeman

area, earn, fame, fare, farm, fear, fern, foam, form, free, frog, from, game, gear, germ, gone, gran, mane, mare, mere, moan, more, name, near, none, rage, rang, rare, rear, roam, roar

Natalie Cole

call, cane, cant, cell, coal, coat, coil, coin, colt, cone, into, lace, lane, late, lean, lent, line, lion, loan, lone, nail, neat, nice, note, once, tail, tale, tall, tell, tile, till, tone

George Foreman

earn, fame, fare, farm, fear, fern, foam, form, free, frog, from, game, gang, gear, germ, gone, gran, mane, mare, mere, moan, moon, more, name, near, rage, rang, rare, rear, roam, roar, roof, room

Bonnie Raitt

bait, bare, barn, bean, bear, beat, bent, bite, boat, bone, bore, born, earn, into, iron, near, neat, nine, none, note, rain, rate, rent, robe, tart, tear, tent, tire, tone, tore, torn

Sally Field

days, deaf, deal, dial, dies, easy, fade, fail, fall, fell, file, fill, fled, idea, idle, lady, laid, lays, lead, leaf, lids, lies, life, safe, said, sail, sale, seal, self, sell, side, slid, yell

Dave Brubeck

acre, back, bake, bare, bark, bead, beak, bear, beer, cake, card, care, cave, crab, cube, curb, cure, dare, dark, dear, deck, deer, duck, duke, ever, race, rack, rake, read, reed, rude, verb

John Dillinger

doll, done, girl, gold, gone, grin, held, hell, herd, hero, hide, hill, hind, hire, hold, hole, horn, idle, iron, join, lend, line, lion, lone, long, lord, nine, none, ride, ring, role, roll

Charles Schulz

acre, arch, call, care, cars, case, cash,
cell, clue, cure, each, ears, hall, haul,
haze, hear, hell, hers, hush, lace, less,
race, real, rule, rush, sale, scar, seal,
seas, sell, such, sure, uses, zeal

Marlo Thomas

also, arms, arts, atom, halt, harm, hats,
host, last, loom, lost, lots, mars, mast,
math, mats, most, moth, oars, oath, oats,
oral, rats, roam, room, root, salt, shot,
slot, solo, sort, star, tool

Kenny Loggins

eggs, goes, gone, inks, keys, king, legs,
lens, lies, like, line, link, lion, logs, lone,
long, lose, nine, none, nose, oils, ones,
only, sign, silk, sing, sink, skin, soil, song,
yolk

Steffi Graf

ages, arts, ears, east, eats, fair, fare, fast,
fate, fear, fire, fist, fits, gate, gear, gets,
gift, raft, rage, rags, rate, rats, rest, rise,
safe, seat, site, star, stir, tear, teas, ties,
tire

Blaise Pascal

able, ball, base, bass, bell, bill, cabs, call,
caps, case, cell, clap, clip, ices, lace,
leap, less, lies, lips, pace, pail, pale, pass,
peas, pies, pile, sail, sale, seal, seas, sell,
slap, slip

Benny Goodman

aged, band, bang, bead, beam, bean,
bend, body, bond, bone, bony, boom,
deny, dome, done, game, gone, good,
made, mane, many, mend, moan, mode,
mood, moon, name, none, noon, obey,
yoga

Zubin Mehta

aunt, bait, bath, beam, bean, beat, bent,
bite, hate, haze, heat, hint, hunt, item,
main, mane, mate, math, meat, mine,
name, neat, tame, team, than, them, then,
thin, time, tube, tune, unit

Daniel Boone

able, band, bead, bean, been, bend, boil,
bold, bond, bone, deal, dial, done, idea,
idle, laid, land, lane, lead, lean, lend, line,
lion, load, loan, lone, nail, need, nine,
none, noon

Tanya Tucker

acre, area, aunt, cake, cane, cant, care, cart, cure, cute, earn, near, neat, neck, race, rack, rake, rank, rate, rent, take, tank, tart, tear, tent, tray, true, tune, turn, yarn, year

Walter Matthau

area, halt, harm, hate, haul, hear, heat, hurt, lame, late, male, mare, mate, math, meal, meat, melt, mule, rate, real, rule, tale, tame, tart, team, tear, term, that, them, true, warm, wear, what

Brigham Young

army, bang, barn, bony, born, burn, bury, gain, gang, grab, gran, gray, grim, grin, hair, hang, harm, horn, hour, hung, hymn, iron, main, many, moan, rain, rang, ring, roam, ruin, rung, yarn, yoga, your

Desmond Tutu

does, dome, done, dots, dune, dust, ends, mend, mode, most, must, nest, nets, nose, note, nuts, ones, send, sent, some, stem, stun, tend, tens, tent, test, toes, tone, tons, tune, unto, used

Guy Lombardo

army, body, bold, boom, bury, door, drag, drug, drum, dumb, glad, goal, gold, good, grab, gray, lady, lamb, load, loom, lord, loud, mold, mood, odor, oral, road, roam, room, ugly, yard, yoga, your

Loretta Lynn

earn, lane, late, lean, lent, loan, lone, near, neat, none, note, only, oral, rate, real, rely, rent, role, roll, tale, tall, tart, tear, tell, tent, tone, tore, torn, tray, yarn, year, yell

Marvin Gaye

area, army, earn, envy, gain, game, gave, gear, germ, give, gran, gray, grim, grin, main, mane, many, mare, mine, name, navy, near, rage, rain, rang, ring, vain, vary, vein, very, vine, yarn, year

Cheryl Tiegs

city, else, eyes, gets, girl, heel, here, hers, hire, hits, ices, legs, lets, lies, list, rely, rest, rice, rich, rise, sigh, site, slit, stir, thee, they, this, ties, tile, tire, tree,

Warren Beatty

area, away, bare, barn, bean, bear, beat, been, beer, bent, earn, near, neat, rare, rate, rear, rent, tart, tear, tent, tray, tree, want, warn, wear, went, were, yarn, yawn, year

Jasper Johns

earn, ears, heap, hear, hens, hero, hers, hope, hops, horn, hose, jars, near, nose, oars, ones, open, pans, pass, pear, peas, pens, rope, rose, seas, shoe, shop, snap, soap, sons, sore, span

George Harrison

aging, agree, anger, arise, arose, eager, error, gains, gears, going, goose, grain, green, grins, hairs, hangs, hears, honor, horns, horse, irons, noise, organ, rains, raise, range, reign, reins, rings, roars, share, sheer, shine, shone

Alan Shepard

ahead, areas, dares, deals, hands, heads, heard, hears, helps, herds, lands, lanes, leads, leaps, learn, lends, panel, pearl, pears, pedal, phase, plane, plans, reads, salad, shade, shape, share, sharp, spade, spare, spear, spend

Calvin Coolidge

alien, alive, alone, along, angel, angle, avoid, caged, canoe, civil, clean, cling, cocoa, dance, devil, doing, given, glide, glove, ideal, legal, lined, lived, local, lodge, loved, novel, ocean, oiled, olive, video, vocal, voice

Count Basie

about, acute, aunts, bacon, basic, basin, beans, beast, beats, bites, boats, bones, cabin, canoe, cause, coast, coats, coins, cones, count, cubes, noise, notes, ocean, ounce, sauce, scent, scout, since, stone, tones, tubes, tunes, units, untie

Waylon Jennings

alien, alone, along, angel, angle, annoy, enjoy, gains, gales, goals, jeans, joins, lanes, lawns, linen, lines, lions, lying, nails, nanny, newly, nines, noise, noisy, nosey, nylon, snail, snowy, swing, wages, wagon, wings, yawns

Smokey Robinson

bikes, bones, books, broke, brook, broom, inner, irons, knobs, miner, minor, money, moons, moose, nines, noise, noisy, noses, nosey, obeys, onion, reins, rinks, rises, robes, robin, rooms, roses, sinks, skies, skins, smoke

George Lucas

acres, agree, argue, arose, cages, cares, cargo, cause, clear, close, clues, coals, coral, cruel, curls, eager, eagle, easel, gales, gauge, gears, glare, glues, goals, grace, large, loser, races, rules, sauce, scale, scare, score, solar, sugar

Sigmund Freud

dried, drugs, drums, dunes, ferns, finds, finer, fired, fires, fried, fries, fumes, funds, germs, grief, grind, grins, guide, mends, minds, mined, miner, minus, nurse, reign, reins, rides, ridge, rings, ruins, rungs, under, urged, using

Humphrey Bogart

about, argue, armor, berry, bumpy, earth, empty, graph, great, group, heart, humor, hurry, marry, maybe, mayor, merry, mouth, opera, other, ought, outer, party, rhyme, rough, route, tempo, thumb, thump, tough, tramp, youth

Elizabeth Taylor

alert, belly, birth, blaze, early, earth, habit, heart, hello, hilly, hotel, label, labor, later, layer, liter, loyal, orbit, other, rally, ratio, relay, royal, table, teeth, their, there, three, title, total, trail, treat, trial, tribe, zebra

Marie Osmond

aimed, arise, armed, arose, aside, dares, domes, doors, drain, dream, ideas, irons, maids, means, mends, mimes, minds, mined, miner, minor, moods, moons, moose, named, names, noise, radio, rains, raise, reads, reins, rides, roads, roman, rooms

Alexander Graham Bell

agree, ahead, alarm, angel, anger, angle, armed, badge, beard, began, blade, blame, blend, brand, bread, drama, dream, eager, eagle, elder, glare, grade, grand, green, heard, label, large, learn, ledge, legal, medal, named, radar, range, relax

Walter Payton

alert, alone, apart, apron, aware, early, entry, later, layer, learn, lower, newly, opera, owner, panel, party, pearl, plane, plant, plate, polar, power, relay, reply, royal, total, towel, tower, treat, water, weary, wrote

Linda Ronstadt

atlas, drain, irons, lands, lions, loads, lords, nails, radio, rails, rains, ratio, roads, roast, salad, slant, snail, solar, solid, stair, stand, start, tails, tarts, tidal, toads, toast, total, trail, train, trial

Abigail Van Buren

again, alien, alive, angel, anger, angle, argue, began, begin, begun, being, bible, brain, brave, bring, given, glare, grain, grave, inner, large, learn, linen, liver, lunar, naval, range, reign, rival, urban, vague, value

Ingrid Bergman

aging, aimed, anger, armed, badge, beard, began, begin, being, brain, brand, bread, bride, bring, drain, dream, drier, grade, grain, grand, grind, image, inner, mined, miner, named, range, reign, rider, ridge, rigid

Neil Sedaka

alien, alike, ankle, aside, asked, deals, dense, easel, ideal, ideas, kinds, knees, lakes, lands, lanes, leads, lends, liked, likes, lined, lines, links, nails, naked, needs, salad, skied, sleek, slide, snail, snake, sneak

Woody Guthrie

dirty, dough, eight, guide, hired, other, ought, outer, ridge, right, rough, route, their, third, threw, throw, tiger, tired, tough, tower, tried, urged, weigh, weird, white, wider, width, wired, worth, write, wrote, youth

Aristotle

alert, arise, arose, later, least, liter, loser, rails, raise, rates, ratio, roast, solar, stair, stare, start, state, steal, stole, store, tails, tales, tarts, taste, tears, tiles, tires, title, toast, total, trail, treat, trial, tries

Dennis Hopper

dense, drops, herds, hides, hired, hoped, hopes, horns, horse, inner, irons, needs, nines, noise, opens, peeps, phone, pines, pipes, ponds, pride, reeds, reins, rides, ripen, roped, ropes, sheep, sheer, shine, shone, speed, spend, spine

Candice Bergen

agree, anger, badge, beard, began, begin, being, brain, brand, bread, bride, bring, cabin, caged, cared, cigar, crane, cried, dance, drain, eager, grace, grade, grain, grand, green, grind, inner, nicer, raced, range, reign, ridge

Richard Simmons

acids, armor, cards, chain, chair, charm, china, choir, chord, coins, comma, cords, crash, cross, disco, drain, hairs, hands, harms, horns, irons, maids, march, marsh, minds, minor, oasis, radio, rains, ranch, roads, roars, roman, sands

Howard Hughes

argue, arose, dares, dough, draws, drugs, gears, grade, grows, guard, harsh, heads, heard, hears, herds, horse, hours, house, reads, roads, rough, shade, share, sugar, swear, sword, urged, wages, wears, whose, words, worse

Rod Stewart

arose, arrow, dares, dates, draws, order, rates, reads, roads, roars, roast, stare, start, state, store, straw, swear, sword, tarts, taste, tears, toads, toast, tower, trade, treat, waste, water, wears, words, worse, worst, wrote

Steven Seagal

agent, angel, angle, atlas, eagle, easel, eaten, elves, event, gales, gases, gates, geese, glass, lanes, lasts, least, leave, naval, nests, sales, saves, seals, seats, sense, seven, slant, slave, stage, steal, steel, tales, tease, tense, vases

Norman Rockwell

allow, alone, ankle, armor, arrow, awoke, camel, canoe, clean, clear, clerk, cloak, clown, color, coral, crane, crawl, cream, crown, known, learn, lemon, local, lower, maker, moral, ocean, owner, roman, woman, women, wreck

Chapter 9: Providers

Provider 1

R	E	P		B	A	R	B		G	O	L	D
O	A	R		A	L	E	E		A	R	I	A
C	U	E		L	A	S	E		T	A	R	P
	S	A	L	S	A		C	E	D	E	S	
R	I	A	L	S		L	O	O	S			
U	R	G	E		P	E	R	T		P	A	S
S	I	E	S	T	A		L	E	A	R	N	T
E	S	S		E	R	N	E		N	O	T	A
		T	A	T	E		C	A	T	E	R	
A	C	M	E	S		A	R	O	S	E		
L	O	A	N		E	R	O	S		S	H	H
T	O	Y	S		R	E	S	T		T	A	O
S	L	O	E		A	R	E	S		S	E	E

Provider 2

S	O	S		S	E	C	S		A	P	O	D
A	R	E		L	O	O	P		S	A	R	I
T	E	E		A	N	N	A		S	L	A	G
	S	P	A	T		S	A	E				
	P	S	S	T		S	T	A	B	S		
L	O	S	E		O	A	K	S		S	E	A
A	N	E	S		R	I	A		C	E	E	S
N	E	T		S	E	L	L		O	A	T	S
E	S	T	E	R		S	E	E	D			
		N	I	P			S	A	P	S		
S	H	A	D		A	D	O	S		H	O	T
P	A	G	E		L	U	X	E		A	L	A
A	P	E	D		S	O	Y	S		T	O	R

Provider 3

S	C	A	T		A	R	M		A	S	P	S
L	O	N	E		L	O	O		S	H	E	A
A	R	T	S		P	O	D		S	E	A	L
T	E	A	T			T	E	L	E			
		A	S	P			E	S	T	O	P	
A	R	C		P	O	R	T	S		O	L	E
L	I	E		A	L	I	A	S		D	I	N
L	O	P		R	O	B	L	E		S	O	T
S	T	E	T	S		L	E	T				
			E	E	L	S		S	A	D	E	
A	M	P	S		A	H	A		A	R	E	A
R	O	U	T		M	I	X		R	I	M	S
T	A	G	S		A	N	E		S	L	O	T

Provider 4

H	U	T		T	R	O	T		O	H	S	
E	T	A	S		A	E	R	O		L	E	A
M	A	N	O		S	E	E	R		D	A	M
		L	A	S	S		T	A	S	T	E	
M	A	T	E	R		P	S	I				
A	G	O		B	A	B	A		L	A	B	S
S	U	M		S	C	A	R	S		P	I	U
T	E	E	D		M	A	S	H		E	K	E
		O	S	E		M	A	R	E	S		
T	A	C	E	T		S	T	O	W			
A	L	E		A	L	O	E		L	A	P	S
P	A	N		R	I	C	E		S	T	O	A
S	E	T		T	S	K	S		T	I	C	

Provider 5

T	H	E		L	O	W	E		S	I	R	E
A	I	R		A	W	A	Y		H	O	A	R
E	N	G		S	E	R	E		A	N	T	S
	T	O	P	E		S	O	L				
		A	R	C	S		S	T	A	F	F	
S	T	A	T		H	A	T	E		B	O	O
H	O	N		G	I	R	O	S		B	E	N
O	N	S		L	A	I	R		B	E	S	T
P	E	A	S	E		S	O	R	A			
		E	E	L			E	T	H	S		
M	E	A	T		A	M	A	S		A	L	B
A	L	I	T		D	O	G	E		S	U	E
E	L	M	S		S	W	A	T		T	E	L

Provider 6

A	I	L	S		A	W	L		C	H	I	N
B	R	I	T		P	I	A		L	A	M	E
S	E	T	A		S	T	Y		A	L	A	N
		R	U	E			S	O	M	E		
A	P	S	E	S		E	R	R	S			
T	I	E		A	L	L	E	E		T	W	A
O	C	A		B	E	A	S	T		S	I	R
M	A	R		L	A	T	H	E		A	R	K
		M	E	R	E		A	C	R	E	S	
A	C	H	E			B	R	R				
L	O	O	T		E	R	E		A	T	O	P
T	I	N	E		T	O	T		S	O	D	A
O	L	E	S		H	E	S		S	E	E	M

Provider 7

A	L	B	S		S	O	W	S		T	W	O
T	A	U	T		A	G	E	E		H	O	W
E	T	N	A		B	E	E	N		A	V	E
		T	H	E	E		S	A	T	E	S	
S	C	R	E	E			T	E	D			
C	O	O		L	O	D	E		S	A	N	E
A	M	P		L	U	R	E	S		R	E	G
D	E	E	D		T	Y	N	E		M	A	G
		O	R	S		C	A	S	T	S		
P	A	S	T	E		M	A	T	E			
O	U	T		S	H	A	Y		D	A	D	O
P	R	O		T	A	L	E		E	L	A	N
S	A	P		S	H	E	S		S	T	Y	E

Provider 8

B	R	O		B	E	N	T		B	A	L	E
R	I	D		A	L	A	R		L	I	E	N
A	P	E		S	K	E	E		A	D	D	S
G	E	S	T	E		E	L	S				
		O	R	T	S		A	T	L	A	S	
C	A	S	E		I	L	K	S		A	N	A
A	W	E	S		L	E	I		L	I	O	N
T	O	M		S	E	E	N		I	N	N	S
S	L	I	C	E		T	E	S	T			
		A	N	T		T	E	M	P	S		
O	W	N	S		E	P	E	E		Y	E	A
H	O	O	T		N	A	V	E		T	R	Y
M	O	T	E		S	P	E	D		H	I	S

Provider 9

S	H	A	H		O	R	B	S		O	H	O
L	I	M	A		D	E	A	N		B	A	R
I	D	E	M		D	A	T	A		O	R	C
D	E	N	S	E		S	O	R	B	E	T	S
			A	T	O	N	E	R				
O	F	F		S	I	N		E	F	F	S	
A	R	I	S	E	S		F	R	E	E	L	Y
F	O	R	E		B	O	A		N	U	N	
		A	G	R	E	E	S					
T	A	S	T	I	E	R		P	L	A	T	S
A	M	I		F	L	A	P		A	G	O	N
M	I	D		T	I	T	I		M	I	N	I
P	E	E		S	T	E	T		P	O	S	T

Provider 10

O	R	T		P	R	E	P		P	I	P	S
D	E	Y		A	I	R	Y		A	M	A	H
D	A	P		S	P	A	R		S	P	R	Y
S	P	E	N	T		S	E	E	S			
			U	S	E		B	E	S	T	S	
P	F	F	T		C	O	B	B		H	U	H
L	E	E		C	H	A	O	S		O	B	I
E	A	T		R	O	T	O		S	O	A	P
D	R	A	P	E		B	R	A				
		O	W	L	S		I	D	L	E	S	
I	S	M	S		A	L	B	A		A	W	E
L	O	U	T		R	A	I	N		D	E	W
L	U	G	S		S	P	O	T		E	R	N

Provider 11

O	F	F	S		C	H	I	S		B	E	T
P	E	A	T		A	U	N	T		R	A	W
S	Y	N	E		P	E	K	E		A	V	A
		A	L	S		N	O	T	E	S		
S	A	B	L	E		P	R	O	A			
P	R	Y		G	L	U	E		R	A	F	T
I	C	E	S		A	M	A		S	A	L	E
N	O	S	E		T	A	R	T		H	E	T
		A	C	E	S		E	A	S	E	S	
B	A	S	S	O		M	A	N				
I	C	E		L	O	G	E		G	N	A	T
E	R	R		T	O	O	T		S	O	N	E
R	E	F		S	H	O	E		T	W	I	N

Provider 12

M	I	N	D		E	M	S		B	E	R	G
A	L	O	W		R	A	N		A	G	H	A
T	I	R	E		G	N	U		R	O	O	M
T	A	M	E		A	G	A	R				
			B	U	R	G		R	I	F	T	S
C	A	W		N	E	E		M	E	L	E	E
I	R	I	S	E	S		P	A	R	A	D	E
T	I	N	E	A		D	I	D		T	S	K
E	D	G	E	S		R	E	A	M			
		R	E	P	O		A	C	T	S		
A	B	L	E		U	G	H		S	O	I	L
F	O	Y	S		R	U	M		T	O	R	A
T	Y	E	S		R	E	M		S	N	O	W

Provider 13

```
E F T   S P A N   C A R D
D I E   L E N O   U V E A
G A R   A N D S   B E N D
E T N A S       P E S T S
      C H A R G E
B A B E   G I R T   S P Y
A B O   O G L E S   H I E
L A D   P I L E   B A G S
      T E E N S Y
W A S P S       T E M P T
H E A R   B A K E   O U R
Y O G I   A N I L   O P E
S N A G   D Y N E   R A Y
```

Provider 14

```
E N D   A N T I   A B R I
W A Y   R E I N   B R A D
E Y E D R O P S   B A N E
    R A N T   H E E D S
M I C A S   O P E S
E L H I   D E E R   S K I
S E A N C E   C O S T A R
H A D   L A G S   L U N K
    S O L I   C O D E S
S E W E D   G R O G
L Y R E   W O O D S M A N
I R E D   A L M A   E Y E
P E N S   S O P S   D E B
```

Provider 15

```
M O C   T A M S   W H A
H I E S   W R A P   H A S
O L L A   O S S A   I R K
    T A S   C O T E S
T R I E R   S H E D
A A S   F L O E   S A C S
N I L   S A L E S   I L K
S L E D   C O L A   D U I
    U S E S   G R E E T
C A D E T   G O A
O V A   O G R E   P A V E
C O W   W H E E   S A I L
A W N   S I B S   H A M
```

We Have
EVERYTHING®
on Anything!

With more than 19 million copies sold, **the Everything® series** has become one of America's favorite resources for solving problems, learning new skills, and organizing lives. Our brand is not only recognizable—it's also welcomed.

The series is a hand-in-hand partner for people who are ready to tackle new subjects—like you!

For more information on the Everything® series, please visit *www.adamsmedia.com*

The Everything® list spans a wide range of subjects, with more than 500 titles covering 25 different categories:

Business	History	Reference
Careers	Home Improvement	Religion
Children's Storybooks	Everything Kids	Self-Help
Computers	Languages	Sports & Fitness
Cooking	Music	Travel
Crafts and Hobbies	New Age	Wedding
Education/Schools	Parenting	Writing
Games and Puzzles	Personal Finance	
Health	Pets	